D0435193

IN THE KITCHEN WITH THE
PIKE PLACE
FISH GUYS

IN THE KITCHEN WITH THE
PIKE PLACE

100 RECIPES AND TIPS FROM THE WORLD-FAMOUS CREW OF PIKE PLACE FISH

Photography by Morgan Keuler

FISH GUYS

WORLD FAMOUS
PIKE PLACE FISH MARKET

THE CREW OF
PIKE PLACE FISH,
BRYAN JARR, & LESLIE MILLER

VIKING STUDIO

VIKING STUDIO

Published by the Penguin Group
Penguin Group (USA) Inc., 375 Hudson Street,
New York, New York 10014, U.S.A.

Penguin Group (Canada), 90 Eglinton Avenue East, Suite 700, Toronto, Ontario, Canada M4P 2Y3
(a division of Pearson Penguin Canada Inc.)

Penguin Books Ltd, 80 Strand, London WC2R 0RL, England

Penguin Ireland, 25 St. Stephen's Green, Dublin 2, Ireland (a division of Penguin Books Ltd)

Penguin Group (Australia), 707 Collins Street, Melbourne, Victoria 3008, Australia
(a division of Pearson Australia Group Pty Ltd)

Penguin Books India Pvt Ltd, 11 Community Centre, Panchsheel Park, New Delhi – 110 017, India

Penguin Group (NZ), 67 Apollo Drive, Rosedale, Auckland 0632, New Zealand
(a division of Pearson New Zealand Ltd)

Penguin Books (South Africa), Rosebank Office Park, 181 Jan Smuts Avenue, Parktown North 2193, South Africa

Penguin China, B7 Jiaming Center, 27 East Third Ring Road North, Chaoyang District, Beijing 100020, China

Penguin Books Ltd, Registered Offices: 80 Strand, London WC2R 0RL, England

First published in 2013 by Viking Studio, a member of Penguin Group (USA) Inc.

10 9 8 7 6 5 4 3 2 1

Copyright © Mukmuk LLC, 2013

All rights reserved

Photograph on page 12 by Stephen Cysewski.

Other photographs by Morgan Keuler. Copyright © Morgan Keuler, 2013.

Line drawings by Nick Jurich, Flashpoint Design.

ISBN 978-0-670-78552-0

Printed in USA

Set in ITC Kabel Std and Sabon Lt Std

Designed by Renato Stanisic

No part of this book may be reproduced, scanned, or distributed in any printed or electronic form without
permission. Please do not participate in or encourage piracy of copyrighted materials in violation of the
author's rights. Purchase only authorized editions.

ALWAYS LEARNING   PEARSON

We Dedicate This Book to
Everyone Who Supports and Inspires Us on Our Journey
Toward Peace and Prosperity for All.

CONTENTS

PART I
BEHIND THE SCENES AT PIKE PLACE FISH

PART II
A (VERY BRIEF) SEAFOOD EDUCATION

PART III
RECIPES

PART I

BEHIND THE SCENES AT PIKE PLACE FISH

INTRODUCTION

or years, decades even, you have found us, the crew of world-
famous Pike Place Fish, in the heart of Seattle's bustling public market
doing our thing. Next to the fresh flower stalls, and the vegetable
stands, and the handmade belts and hats, we throw (and catch!) a lot of
salmon. We fillet halibut, pack mussels, and clean crabs to be cracked open in
Seattle kitchens and also to be flown to Idaho, Kansas, and Oklahoma, too.
We spook customers with an "attack fish" on a string (adults always jump
more than the kids), then enjoy a good laugh together. We give a lot of hugs,
mug for a lot of snapshots, and sell a lot of great seafood.

But our "thing" isn't any one of those things; in fact, our "thing" is even
more than the sum of all its parts. This thing we believe in more than
anything else is making a connection with each and every person who stops in
to Pike Place Fish and really touching the life of our customers, whether
they're buying or not. With every person we talk to, we have a new
opportunity to improve someone's day, to teach someone how to store or

OPPOSITE: If the throw is all in the wrist, the catch is all in the biceps!

The historic Pike Place Market, where Pike Place Fish is located, has terrific wares and great energy.

handle the fish they're buying, or educate someone on why making ocean-friendly choices actually makes a difference. We do this when we hand out tastes of salmon jerky to people curious to try this unusual treat and when we sell crab cocktails for people to eat while they navigate the waterfront crowds. Yet every day we hear the same simple question from our customers as we wrap their halibut, salmon, shrimp, crabs, and mussels: "How do I cook this?" Whether the seafood they have chosen is totally unfamiliar or the customer is just tired of the same old recipe, we are continually pressed for our favorite ways to prepare seafood. For years, people have been asking us to put out a cookbook compiling them all.

We all have our own go-to recipes that we've been sharing with customers for years. We each have tips and tricks and shortcuts for busy folks, for families with kids, for customers looking to branch out or angling for a great company dish. But now that we've gone totally sustainable—carrying only fish and seafood whose harvest promotes healthy, diverse oceans—we feel as if there was a reason we haven't done the cookbook until now. Not only can we share recipes, which is fun and awesome, but we get another venue for helping people "get" what sustainability is all about. We get to do what we love and talk about why it matters what fish we sell, and which you buy and eat. We also realize that as much as we love touching the lives of the people who come through Pike Place Fish or who order from us online or call in, we are thrilled to have the opportunity to connect with so many more people, people who might not ever make it out to Seattle but who will read this book. We want you to think of us as ambassadors (even though we wear orange overalls instead of suits): ambassadors of sustainable food systems, ambassadors

Yori doing what he loves best—sharing salmon jerky samples with the crowd.

We love our customers!

of Seattle and our rockin' West Coast lifestyle, ambassadors of a commitment to integrity *and* fun, and ambassadors of Pacific salmon, Alaskan halibut and spot prawns, Dungeness crab, and so much more!

This book also introduces you to recipes from longtime customers, and from the businesses and restaurants we supply and are surrounded by at the Pike Place Market, all of whom enjoy great seafood just as much as we do. We do this because Pike Place Fish is more than just a business that sells seafood—it is a community that interacts with and affects everyone who it touches. This cherished belief helped make Pike Place Fish the "world famous" fish market it is today, as did you, our loyal customers.

We thought a lot about what went into this book. We tested and retested each and every recipe, and included only those that knocked our socks off. We tried to give you as many chances as possible to work healthy, delicious seafood into your day. Start with a crab quiche at breakfast and at sunset end with Alaskan king crab legs on the grill. We tried and tested and tasted scores of basic recipes for chowders and crab cakes and all the standards, and included only the ones that either offered us something new or represented a traditional recipe as solidly as a classic should. We know what it's like to need to feed a family, and we've included recipes kids will happily eat that can also be prepared in a flash, even on a weeknight. And the influence of different cultures and our families' culinary heritages is seen on every page, from Japanese-style miso soup with clams to Caribbean seafood chowder to Filipino-style squid. You have always been able to buy our delicious rubs, and now you can also make them at home. Start with great fish, rub it up, then roast or grill it. You've never had better, or simpler, eating. Whether you're a beginner with a lot of questions or an expert looking for new dishes to add to your repertoire, we hope you find just what you need. In short, enjoy! And drop us a line or come by and tell us what you think. This is only the beginning of a whole new relationship with you all, and we couldn't be more excited. Thanks for coming along on our ride.

Former crew member Dan Bugge, owner of Matt's in the Market, talking oysters with Jake.

THE LOST ART OF THE FISHMONGER: IT'S THE CONNECTION THAT MATTERS

There are a lot of tourists who come through Seattle's Pike Place Market on any given day, even when the Seattle skies are living up to their reputation and basting people in a damp drizzle as they walk by on the cobblestone street in front of the shop. And we're not exaggerating when we say *a lot*: the Market draws about ten million visitors annually and is the focus of more snapshots than that kooky tower rising like a spaceship out of the base of Queen Anne Hill (we refer to the Space Needle, of course).

It is sometimes hard to see behind the visitors posing in front of the original Starbucks, or kissing a salmon over here at our Pike Place Fish storefront, but the core of the Market isn't about any particular stall, nor is it about the coffee, the flowers, or even the salmon. After all, you can buy any of these things at the grocery store. What's behind the crowds is the kind of active, vibrant public space that's been all but lost in modern life. It's a chance to tap your foot to the tune the busker is playing on the piano improbably rolled to the street corner. It's the opportunity to talk with a farmer about the weather over bouquets of sweet peas, and an invitation to sample a slice of heirloom apple or a taste of smoked fish before you buy. It's like an old-time village square come alive again. And no one knows that better than we do. We've been in conversation with the crowds since 1965, and we've enjoyed every minute of it.

Pike Place Fish has built its reputation and business on more than the fish and seafood out on display, and on more than the 1.5 million pounds of seafood we sell every year. Loyal customers and the curious alike throng to our booth because it's more than the fish they want to take home. For the same reason people crave buying produce through neighborhood farmers' markets, it can be incredibly rewarding to buy fish and shellfish through a fishmonger. If it's not us, maybe it's one near you in New York, or Orlando,

MEET YOUR FISHMONGER
JAISON SCOTT: YEARS AS A FISHMONGER: 19 FAVORITE SEAFOOD: SPOT PRAWNS

HOW IT ALL BEGAN: FIFTY YEARS OF PIKE PLACE FISH

Today, vendors sell fruit in the spot where Pike Place Fish owner John Yokoyama's dad first opened a produce stand in 1950, right next to where Pike Place Fish stands in Seattle. In 1963, Johnny began working at the market as one of several employees of a quiet, unassuming little fish stand. After numerous unsuccessful attempts to sell the business, John's employer offered him the opportunity to purchase Pike Place Fish. As a young man of twenty-five, John was at first hesitant to buy the business, but he ultimately decided he could do better on an owner's salary. In 1965, snapper cost 29 cents a pound, and the going price for Pike Place Fish was $3,500.

In the first few years of owning the market, times were tough. Fishermen and wholesalers gathered at the piers edging Puget Sound, hawking their catch. With not a dime to spare, the enterprising Johnny negotiated with the

From left to right: longtime PPF employee Charles Hanoh; original owner, Bill Constantine; and future owner, John Yokoyama, circa 1964.

wholesalers to let him pay on terms, which gave him some time to sell his product before he paid them out. For the first six years, Johnny manned the fish stall six days a week, with just one employee to help him out.

In the 1980s, Johnny knew something needed to change. While the fish market had grown, turnover was high and morale was low. Johnny brought on business consultant Jim Bergquist on a three-month trial to help the business reinvent itself and find success. Together, Johnny and our whole crew decided our goal was to become "world famous." We didn't want to accomplish our goal through any advertising. We simply started with extraordinary customer service and a commitment to making a difference to each visitor. Once we put that energy out there, it came back to us in spades.

We participated in the Goodwill Games, had a bit spot in the 1993 movie *Free Willy*, and chatted it up on *Good Morning America*. We were the focus of newspaper articles, made the cut for Spike Lee's Levi's commercial, and got our mugs plastered across national magazine spreads. We were world famous!

MEET YOUR FISHMONGER

JOHN YOKOYAMA:

YEARS AS A FISHMONGER: 50

FAVORITE SEAFOOD: KING SALMON

Then Dicky Yokoyama, Johnny's brother, had an idea for Pike Place Fish: the Movie. Some of you might have seen our training film that describes the business philosophy and practices that made us great. We started touring the country doing presentations, too—a total honor that we are jazzed to be able to do. We love sharing the love! Now that we're known the world over, we've set our sights on nothing less than "World Peace and Prosperity for All," and we can't wait to see what the next fifty years bring.

MEET YOUR FISHMONGER

DICK YOKOYAMA:

YEARS AS A FISHMONGER: 36

FAVORITE SEAFOOD: ALBACORE TUNA

MEET YOUR FISHMONGERS: TWO RYANS!

RYAN RECTOR (LEFT): YEARS AS A FISHMONGER: 8 FAVORITE SEAFOOD: OYSTERS

RYAN YOKOYAMA (RIGHT): YEARS AS A FISHMONGER: 6 FAVORITE SEAFOOD: HALIBUT CHEEKS

or San Francisco. So what is all the fuss about working with a fishmonger? What do you get out of the deal that you don't get by selecting a wrapped piece of fish from a display case at the supermarket? Well, besides our roguish charm and boyish good looks, we think there are three primary benefits to working with a fishmonger.

RELATIONSHIPS

Our daily lives are made up of a series of small moments and interactions, from those with our families and the people around us to interactions out there in the business world, whether we're closing a big deal, giving directions to someone who's lost, ordering a sandwich at a deli, or picking up a package at the post office. If each of us makes a commitment to come to every one of these interactions, no matter how small, with great intent and an attitude of generosity, then all that good feeling just expands out into the world. It's the way our team works at Pike Place Fish, and maybe it's part of the reason that as a nation we seem to be swinging back to an old-fashioned corner store approach to shopping, even in bigger cities like Seattle. You can get your milk delivered to your door, stop by the butcher for a cut of meat, select your vegetables at the fruit stand, and buy a beautiful piece of fish from the fishmonger. It takes time, and it isn't always practical when you've got a to-do list a mile long. But part of the reward comes from the fact that buying food this way requires care and effort, and the effort itself elevates food from something cheap and convenient to something you care about a good deal more. The food itself remains a critical part of the equation, and the relationship with the person you're buying it from completes the picture. We've found from talking with scores of customers every day that those relationships offer their own enrichment to daily life, providing these critical human connections we all need.

TRUST

Out of that relationship building comes something critical in this whole food retailer–consumer model: trust. Buying fish from guys you know and like means you don't have to wonder if they are pushing the skunky bits at you, hoping you won't notice until you get home, or passing off haddock as cod. It means they'll take the time to steer you to the right fish for the dish you want to make, even if it's five bucks less a pound than the first one that caught your eye. It means that if a sockeye is marked "wild-caught Alaskan salmon," it didn't come from a farm. For us, it also means that for any fish or clam or crab sitting out on ice we can tell you where it came from and how it was caught, and assure you it came from a healthy fishery. We have incredible pride in the fish and seafood we sell. Nothing makes us prouder than matching you up with the right product. That trust extends from us to you as well. We trust that happy, satisfied customers who are treated well and get great fish become loyal customers. And that keeps Pike Place Fish sustainable.

EXPERTISE

There are several aspects to the expertise fishmongers develop as part of our trade that are of benefit to you. The first is the quality of technique you can rely on when you're in the shop. For example, we fillet salmon every day. If you buy a whole salmon from us and want it broken down, you've got it: steaks, fillets, whole sides. You ask and we'll start sharpening our knives. Need your mackerel gutted? We're your men. Crab cleaned? Done. Think fish scales are machines used for weighing trout? It's okay, we're here to help.

Making your life a little easier is our job. But beyond that, there's the expertise we can convey in education, and we're happy to provide that whether you buy some fish or not. Maybe you don't know why farmed salmon is not a product we sell at Pike Place Fish. Because fish are our business, we can tell you that it takes three pounds of feed to create every pound of weight in a farmed salmon, making it a resource-intensive food to produce. We could add that when farmed salmon lacking the chops to make it in the open sea escape into wild populations and breed, it creates even more risk for the very fish the farmed salmon are meant to protect. It also means we're not reactive to buzzwords. We can assure you that not all farming is bad, and point to the successfully farmed oysters, clams, and mussels that are pulled from the waters surrounding Seattle.

Finally, on a more practical level, maybe you have no idea how to cook squid (either fast and hot or low and slow is the answer) or the difference between a prawn and a shrimp. Whether it's in person, online, or through this book, we're happy to explain. And isn't that a lot more fun than searching for someone to ask while you stand, cold and unsure, in front of wrapped Styrofoam trays? We think it's a no-brainer.

WHY WE WENT SUSTAINABLE: FOOD FOR THOUGHT

n January 2011, our regular customers noticed a change at our storefront in Pike Place Market. The monkfish was gone. Not just monkfish you could buy to take home and eat, but a whole monkfish, hidden in ice, waiting for an unsuspecting customer to pass close by or linger to look over the mussels or the clams. Suddenly, the monkfish would seem to lunge and move its huge, ugly maw (for those of you who don't know what a monkfish looks like, think of a monster from the sea—all big, horrible head). You see, every day we used to tie a monkfish to a string that we controlled in

If you've ever seen us in person or on TV tossing a fish, you might be interested to know more about that salmon you see flying through the air. We buy specific "stunt" salmon just for throwing, and when they are no longer worthy of tossing (after about a hundred tosses they get a little funky), we freeze them. When we have enough, we donate them to Seattle's Woodland Park Zoo and nearby Wolf Haven International to feed the animals. We even get to throw fish to the bears.

Proud to be sustainable.

A proud graduate of the Pike Place Fish salmon-catching school.

back. Kids freaked out, then wanted us to do it again and again. Adults laughed at being scared, if only for a minute. Everyone had a good time. The monkfish was sort of an unofficial mascot, something locals would bring their visiting relatives to see. But that January, the monkfish went away.

Why? Because monkfish are usually caught in a cone-shaped net weighted down by heavy chains and dragged along the seafloor by a boat. This fishing method, known as bottom trawling, rips up the seafloor, damaging the habitat where other fish and sea life need to feed and breed. The nets also catch more than monkfish. Known as bycatch, the other fish and marine animals caught in the nets aren't used for food, or used at all. They are thrown over the boat either already dead or dying. Sometimes monkfish are caught using gillnets, another form of fishing that can catch and kill sea turtles and other marine mammals in addition to fish.

We don't know how this sounds to you, but to us, it didn't sound right. And unsustainable fishing methods didn't sit right with many of our customers either, prompting us to take a good, long look at the issue. We had a lot to learn. But we knew one thing: we love fish, and we want to keep selling fish, and eating it, which means supporting healthy populations in which fish can grow and thrive. We had to invest and learn and educate ourselves about what was what. What we found was a planet of hurting oceans and endangered fish.

The more we found out about the state of our oceans, the more strongly we felt about making a change. We are simply taking out too many fish at a time, and we're damaging breeding habitats at the same time with pollution and structural changes to our coastlines. You'd think that farmed fish—a process known as aquaculture—would be the answer. After all, fish are the last wild animal that we harvest in this way. When we want pork, we don't all go hunt wild boar; we raise pigs. It seems as if raising salmon in pens instead of going after the wild stock would keep the wild populations intact and be more consistent in the catch numbers and more cost effective, too. But farming methods are not yet perfect, and some aquaculture hurts more than it helps. Because we're known for our salmon, let's take the common example of farmed Atlantic salmon. While our own stocks of Pacific salmon here on the

We're not the only ones who love seafood.

West Coast are more plentiful, they are still vulnerable due to logging, the loss of wetlands, and hydroelectric dams barring river access. In order to meet demand, you'd think farmed Atlantic salmon would be the perfect answer. Here's why it isn't.

Farmed salmon incur some of the same problems we hear about related to intensively farmed or "factory-farmed" meat. Animals that are fed concentrated feed specifically meant to bulk them up quickly and are kept in such close proximity, in dense populations, are vulnerable to disease. In the case of salmon, this can take the form of nasty parasites called sea lice. Infected farmed fish can escape and spread disease to wild fish. Or, to get rid

The crew watching firsthand how Penn Cove mussels are harvested.

of the sea lice, the salmon may be treated to pesticide baths that affect the surrounding marine environment and other sea animals, like crab and shrimp. And we haven't even mentioned the problem of all that—how shall we put it so as not to offend—fish "waste" that accumulates in the area, filtering out into the water.

The interbreeding of escaped farmed fish and wild fish is also a problem. Farmed Atlantic salmon, most of which are grown outside the United States and imported, are often raised in net pens set in the same marine environment where wild fish live. Storms or rough waters can damage the pens, allowing fish to escape, which can also happen during everyday operations running the farm. These "escapees" have no sense of being different from their wild cousins and will interbreed with them if given the chance. The resulting offspring are genetically different from the wild stock and are often not well equipped to survive in the wild (otherwise this would be an easy answer to replacing the stocks of Atlantic salmon).

Aquaculture is an idea that makes sense, and done right for some species it's an idea that works. However, in many of the important ways listed above it hasn't proved in all cases to be the perfect solution to providing good alternative fish for food.

In the end, we also didn't feel that unsustainable methods jibe with our ethos and our commitment to world peace. You can't have peace on land and not at sea, right? So we teamed up with the experts at Monterey Bay Aquarium Seafood Watch to guide us toward choices that promote healthy oceans. Seafood Watch makes it easy for consumers by rating seafood as a "Best Choice," "Good Alternative," or something you should "Avoid," and they also tell you why. Some species should be avoided because they've been overfished or are caught or farmed in ways that have an impact on other wildlife or their habitats. Other fish are sustainable if they're caught using

THERE'S AN APP FOR THAT

There are a few programs to choose from that educate people about ocean health and help both businesses and individual consumers make informed choices about the fish they sell, buy, and eat. We chose Seafood Watch because they know their stuff and base their decisions on hard science, but there are lots of other institutes and organizations out there that can help guide you toward more sustainable choices. They include the Blue Ocean Institute, New England Aquarium, FishWise, Seachoice, Ocean Wise, Food Alliance, and National Oceanic and Atmospheric Administration (NOAA) Fisheries' FishWatch. The Marine Stewardship Council (MSC) also operates a global certification program for sustainable fisheries. All of these sources have good information, but their rating systems vary, so you might have to do a little work to figure out the criteria they use and their own coding systems. When you're buying fish from us, it's easy: everything we sell is sustainable. We've done the work for you. But if you're out buying fish from your own fishmonger or even ordering sushi at your favorite spot, making a sustainable choice can be as easy as whipping out your fancy phone.

lines and hooks, but not if they're scooped up in a purse net. Even some aquaculture works great—our nearby oyster, clam, and mussel farms are good examples of that. We like the spirit of supporting good methods and great fishermen, and we like the education component as well. We've learned a lot, and we enjoy passing on what we know to you, making it easy and making it fun. Doing the right thing doesn't have to be all dour and serious. We're serious about our commitment, and feel great about our choice. That's why in January 2011 Pike Place Fish became the first 100 percent sustainable fish market in Washington State.

The word "sustainable" is used so often that it has almost become difficult to define because it means so many different things to different people. When we say we've become 100 percent sustainable, we mean that our buying and selling practices "help sustain wild, diverse and healthy ocean ecosystems that will exist long into the future," which is the definition Seafood Watch developed and operates by. We recognize that fishing choices have power over our oceans, lakes, and streams, and can improve or worsen the size and health of different populations, the condition of the habitats fish and shellfish live in, and how many and how long we'll have fish into the future. Every type of fish we sell is evaluated using the following criteria, to make sure it meets our definition of sustainable:

- **How vulnerable is that specific fish to fishing pressure? Are the numbers dropping too quickly?**
- **How do the numbers look on that fish species right now? Are there enough? Are there enough fish of breeding age?**
- **What is the extent and type of the bycatch, or those untended fish and animals caught when that fish is harvested?**
- **What effect do fishing practices used to harvest that fish have on different habitats and ecosystems?**

This means Pike Place Fish no longer carries some fish at all, like monkfish. We couldn't find any fisheries that met our criteria. In other cases we switched fisheries; for example, switching from Mexican farmed shrimp to wild-caught

MEET YOUR FISHMONGERS

TAHO KAKUTANI (LEFT): YEARS AS A FISHMONGER: 7 FAVORITE SEAFOOD: KING SALMON

CHRIS BELL (RIGHT): YEARS AS A FISHMONGER: 11 FAVORITE SEAFOOD: KING SALMON

shrimp from the United States. In fact, that was a fun and unexpected effect of going sustainable. We found that many U.S. producers were using sustainable methods, while many fisheries in other countries were not. So in making our shift to sustainability, we were also able to go more local and increase the number of U.S. suppliers we buy from. That was a win-win we could really get behind. Not only were we supporting the American economy, but we also limited the distance and resources used to transport the seafood. Sometimes we had to really search far and wide. For example, we found only two sea bass fisheries that met our criteria, in the entire world!

Our initial fears about whether customers would support us through this change proved totally unfounded. In fact, we discovered that once customers

MEET YOUR FISHMONGER
JAKE JARDINE: YEARS AS A FISHMONGER: 4 FAVORITE SEAFOOD: HALIBUT

knew why we made the switch and the reasons behind our not carrying certain items or carrying higher-priced but sustainable products, they flooded us with support. People enjoy doing the right thing, especially when you make it easy to do and easy to understand the reasons behind it. In making Pike Place Fish sustainable, we aimed to make sure our message was clear: we support sustainability because we support fish. And that's not a West Coast thing, or a Seattle thing, or a liberal hippie thing. That's just a smart thing.

BUY SMART

To make fish selection easy, we recommend either buying from a completely sustainable market that uses a rating system you understand and trust or staying abreast of the changing rankings through due diligence (and maybe the help of your smartphone). But at a glance, below we list some of the current Best Choice and Good Alternative selections from the Seafood Watch Guide. These selections are all available at Pike Place Fish, or look for them at your local fish shop. The fine print matters. Start up a conversation and ask about fishing methods and species. For example, Atlantic cod caught by trawlers doesn't make the list. Nor does tilapia farmed in Asia. If you find your local market or fishmonger doesn't sell a sustainable option, ask them to carry it and then buy it when they do. Supporting good business choices with your money and patronage is one of the best ways you as a consumer can effect change in the marketplace and in our oceans.

Wild American shrimp

Alaskan spot prawns

Alaskan halibut

Alaskan red king crabs

Farmed clams

U.S. nontrawled Pacific cod

Dungeness crabs

U.S. Pacific halibut

Farmed mussels

Farmed oysters

Alaskan and Canadian sablefish/black cod

Alaskan wild salmon

U.S. Pacific sardines

Oregon pink shrimp

Farmed tilapia

U.S.-farmed rainbow trout

Canadian and Pacific troll- or pole-caught albacore tuna

U.S.-farmed catfish

Pacific sole

Wild Alaskan scallops

PART II

A (VERY BRIEF) SEAFOOD EDUCATION

If you visit us in Seattle (or order online), we'll carve out your halibut cheeks for you, but in the spirit of education, this section aims to give you just enough information to make you dangerous. We'll share tricks for dealing with the dreaded Fear of Fish Bones, teach you how to fillet a salmon like the experts, tell you how long you can keep your mussels before you cook them, and how to keep them happy while they wait. Part of your seafood primer covers an aspect of sustainability that people don't always talk or think about related to seafood: saving those bones, shells, heads, and collars and using the bits to make really delicious, sustainable, and thrifty meals. Okay, let's get you on your way.

CHOOSING THE RIGHT SEAFOOD FOR YOU AND WHAT TO DO ONCE YOU TAKE YOUR FISH HOME

The best way to get great seafood every time is to choose a quality fishmonger and become a regular. A fishmonger won't steer you wrong; it's in the Fishmonger's Code. Still, it's nice to know a little something about whether you're picking a good piece of fish if one of us isn't picking it out for you. You may have heard about checking the gills to ensure they're bright red, or looking into the fish's eyes. Pike Place Fish manager Sam remembers when we used to get headless salmon (caught with gillnets). Customers freaked out because there were no gills to check. No eyeballs to examine.

What Sam tells people who ask is to use all your senses (and your sense) when you're choosing fish. Take a whiff. If it smells, run. That bell can't be unrung, if you know what we mean.

If it's a whole fish, look to see if it has scales and slime—the protective coating on a fish's skin. Slime is a good thing. Slime and scales tend to rub off when the fish has been iced down too many times, meaning that the fish has been hanging around awhile. If there's blood, it should be red. Fresh blood is red, while old blood is brownish in color.

MEET YOUR FISHMONGER

ANDERS MILLER: YEARS AS A FISHMONGER: 12 FAVORITE SEAFOOD: BLACK COD

If you are buying live crabs and lobsters, the shellfish should be spoiling for a fight. Feisty is good. Especially if you're not the one who has to reach in to get them. We are quite happy the Dungeness beauties we sell are already cooked.

Mussels and clams should be tightly closed. If they're gaping and you flick them with your finger, they should close. If they don't, toss 'em. Oysters should have clear liquor inside, not milky. If it's milky, toss 'em.

SEAFOOD STORAGE

One of the biggest impediments we hear from people who want to eat fish or shellfish more often is that they feel that if they don't consume the fish within two minutes of buying it, it will go bad and they'll be left without dinner and have wasted money to boot. Fresh fish is fabulous. But you have more than a minute, we promise you. Follow the guidelines below and have no fear:

Clams and Mussels

Remove them from the plastic bag as soon as you get home. Place them in a colander set inside a larger bowl. Wet a clean kitchen towel and wring it out a little. Tuck that over the top as if you are tucking in a little baby and put the clams or mussels in the fridge. They'll keep for five days this way if you keep moistening the towel. If any gape and won't close when you flick them, throw them away.

Fish and Cooked Crabs

Fish will keep for three days in the fridge, as will cooked crabs. If you know you won't get to them right away or suddenly have to fly to Mexico, then freeze them instead.

If you find yourself with a whole fish, like a mackerel from our shop or a

HOW WE LIKE TO FREEZE FISH

This method limits the contact your fish has with air, and that's good, because air is the enemy of the frozen fish.

When freezing a fish, always remove it from the bag you brought it home in or unwrap it if it is wrapped in white paper. Place the fish in a resealable plastic bag, preferably a heavier gauge one made for the freezer. Fill a large pot with water and dip the bag below the surface of the water. Wait until all the air bubbles are out, close the bag underwater, then pull it out. You can also put water in the bag, then add the fish, then press out all the air. . . . You see where we're going with this.

If you are not freezing the fish in water, place it in a heavy-duty resealable plastic bag, press out the air, and freeze. Alternatively, if you have a vacuum sealer, it works well, too. Be careful handling the fish in the freezer as vacuum-sealed packages can open if handled roughly and let in air, which is, you remember, the enemy of your fish.

fish you've caught yourself, remember that it's best to clean and gut your fish as soon as possible. The bacteria in the digestive tract of the fish starts to do naughty things once the fish dies, especially if the temperature is warmer. When you buy any fish, always rinse it and pat it dry before using.

WHAT DO YOU RECOMMEND . . . ?

People ask us this all the time, and we all have our favorites. Here are a few suggestions from the crew:

- **Yori always points people toward the smoked salmon or the salmon jerky. People who say they don't "like" fish inhale our smoked salmon. Salmon jerky is a whole lot tastier and better for you as a snack than one of those protein bars, and it keeps like a dream.**

- Kids like stuff they can play with: prawns, tail fillets (boneless), small fish fried whole, mussels and clams, or crab claws. Or make fish fingers, fish cakes, or salmon patties.
- Ryan likes that oysters are very representative of the waters from which they were pulled (if they were wine, you'd call that *terroir*).
- Black cod is also called sablefish for a reason. Jake says people adore the buttery, rich taste.
- For those who find fishy fish suspicious, choose a whitefish like sole, snapper, rockfish, or halibut.
- If you're new to fish, try just using some of the rubs and cooking the fish simply. That way you have flavor and get used to the characteristics of the particular fish you are using.

Interested in seafood that won't break the bank? These are your best bets:

- **OYSTERS. Get a lesson on how to shuck an oyster (or just refer to page 49 for a lesson right now). That way you'll be eating on the half shell for half the price of your favorite oyster bar.**
- **CLAMS AND MUSSELS. Not only are clams and mussels cheap, but you get to play with your food, scooping the meat out of the shells as you go. That type of hands-on eating slows down even the fastest diners, allowing all to truly enjoy the food; kids think it's fun; and dunking bread into the steaming liquid becomes its own course.**
- **SOLE is delicate and great for you, and you can get a dozen fillets for less than a venti latte.**
- **SQUID is a steal and is great fried, sautéed, even stuffed.**
- **LINGCOD is half the price of halibut and has incredible snowy-white flesh.**
- **ROCKFISH. If we were girls, we would call rockfish the little black dress of the fish fillet world.**
- **WHOLE FISH are always more economical than fillets. And cooking and presenting a whole fish impresses people, like the aforementioned girls, perhaps wearing their little black dresses.**

THERE ARE BONES IN MY FISH!

Maybe it's because bone-choking scenes have been featured in too many movies or something, but people really seem to have a fear, an actual fear, of fish bones. Which would make them, wait, osteophobes? This fear is half the reason people buy fillets, hoping they won't have to deal with that dreaded skeleton. Now, we can't say we understand the fear completely, but we understand that it bothers you. And if it bothers you, it bothers us. So let's see what we can do about it.

The most obvious solution is to make your problem our problem. Ask your fishmonger to remove the bones for you if that's doable. With trout and tilapia

MEET YOUR FISHMONGER

RYAN REESE:

YEARS AS A
FISHMONGER: 2

FAVORITE SEAFOOD:
COPPER RIVER
SOCKEYE SALMON

and other fish, your fishmonger can help by doing a "**V-cut**," which is accomplished by making two angled cuts that remove the line of offending bones. Starting a bit out from the center line where the bones are in the fish, angle in and cut down to just under the bones. Repeat on the other side, angling down to meet the other cut and forming a V. You lift out the piece of fish that contains all those bones (and put it in the stockpot).

Filleting a fish removes the spine and the rib bones. Pin bones are intramuscular bones that float in the flesh angling toward the head. Pulling out these bones on your own is easy if you invest in a pair of tweezers or needle-nose pliers. (We can attest to the fact that women do not like it when you "borrow" their tweezers to pull out pin bones. Buy some fish bone tweezers or just use clean pliers.) Using the back of a knife, run it along the fillet toward the tail to raise the tips of the bones. Hold the fillet with one hand and use your other hand to pull out the bones, one by one, at a 45 degree angle toward the head (the wider part of the fillet). Skinless fillets are easier to "pin bone," but on a salmon or other fish with delicious skin, it's not worth skinning it just for that.

Avoid the hassle altogether by selecting tailpieces of fillet. Bones go only so far back on most fish, because the fish have that swishy tail that needs a lot of flexibility to do its job. Tail fillets may be more oddly shaped, but they don't have bones. Fishmonger Reese, a dad himself, says he recommends tailpieces for parents worried about little kids getting a bone in their food.

With some fish, like black cod, the pin bones rise out with the fat when the fish is cooked, making removing them a snap. The same is true with salmon. **Cooking first** makes removing the bones before eating a snap, and it contributes flavor while it cooks.

HOW LONG SHOULD I COOK MY FISH?

Really it is best to err on the side of rarer, remembering that fish will continue to cook once it's off the heat. Fish should just flake when you test with a fork or might show white curds or proteins on the surface.

Shrimp and prawns should just curl and turn opaque. The crabs we sell are already cooked, so remember that when using them in a dish. Cook them just long enough to heat them through. One of the best ways we find to heat crab is to steam it, which helps keep the meat moist. Mussels and clams will have just popped open when they are ready to eat.

THE BENEFITS (AND RISKS) OF EATING SEAFOOD

- In general, seafood is an excellent source of lean protein that is low in saturated fat.
- Seafood, especially salmon, tuna, rainbow trout, sardines, mackerel, herring, and anchovies, is rich in omega-3 fatty acids.
- Omega-3s are the same fatty acids put into capsules and sold as heart-healthy "fish oil." They are widely believed to help lower rates of heart disease, reduce high blood pressure, help relieve arthritis symptoms, and prevent cancer. Hooray for fish!
- However, as we learned doing our sustainability work, some contaminants like mercury, heavy metals (not the music), and other toxins like PCBs and dioxins make their way into the water supply and then into fish. If you eat too much contaminated seafood, it can affect your health. Check with a seafood sustainability program for lists of fish with potentially harmful levels of toxins (See page 23).
- Fish with lower mercury levels include shrimp, salmon, pollack, and catfish. In general, the lower you eat on the food chain, the lower the levels of these substances they are likely to have. In this case, thinking small is actually better.

HOW TO THROW A SALMON

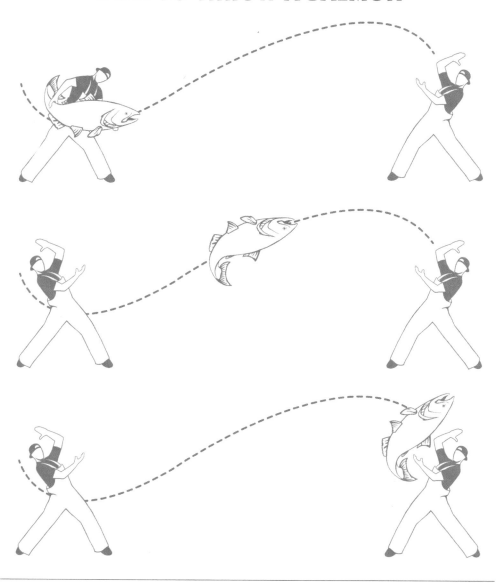

You may have heard the disclaimer "Don't try this at home!" in reference to stunts you see on TV. When it comes to our trademarked fish tossing, we don't agree. In fact, we encourage people to try their hand at throwing fish every day at the market. It's not hard, it's just all in the technique, so we've outlined some of our favorite moves step by step in the book. However, if you're going for more advanced throws like the Oh My God It's a Whole Freaking Halibut toss, we do recommend wearing a back support device. Above you'll find all you need to complete our classic salmon belly twist, a crowd-pleasing favorite.

HOW TO PLAY A FISHMONGER ON TV

You know we'll clean and scale your fish for you, but don't you want to impress your buddies by scaling that trout you just caught, or by cleaning a crab right in front of their eyes? Plus, as much as we'd like to, we can't travel back home in every visitor's suitcase. Here are some tips to carry you through when we can't be by your side.

HOW TO SCALE A FISH

Usually, wherever you buy a whole fish, there is a fishmonger who will scale the fish for you. If there is, have him or her do it. Unless you have a deep sink, you'll have scales flying all over your kitchen. However, you could also scale a fish outdoors.

A tool not made for this purpose but absolutely amazing for scaling fish is a curry comb, the kind used to brush horses. Buy one new (don't use the one from the barn), and keep it clean. It will scale a fish in a hot second. Alternatively, you can use a knife, of course. Some people even make their

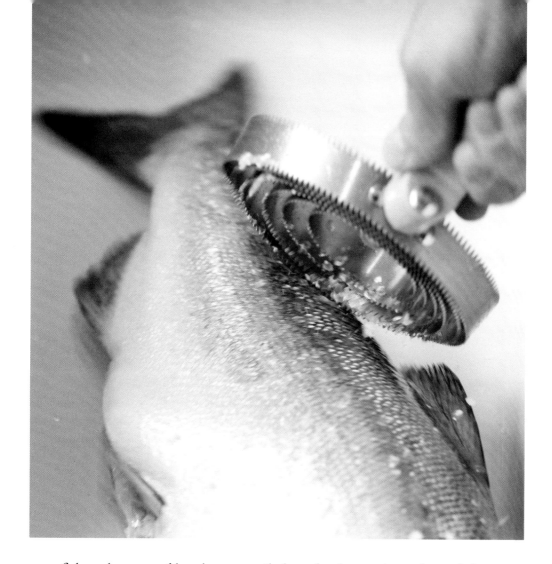

own fish scalers out of bottle caps nailed or glued to a piece of wood that extends down to form a handle. The ridged, sharp edges of the bottle caps do a great job removing scales.

When you're scaling a fish, remember that fish scales scallop back toward the tail. This means that to remove them, you need to work in the other direction, in short, sweeping strokes toward the head. Grab the tail as a handle and, using short strokes, scrape against the direction of the scales. Be careful when working around the fins or toward the belly, where the skin is more delicate. Rinse the fish and use your fingers to run over the fish to ensure you've removed all the scales.

HOW TO FILLET A SALMON

A salmon is what is called a round fish, as opposed to a flat fish like sole. If you know how to fillet a salmon, you know how to fillet any similar fish. This is fishmonger Justin's method. He learned how to fillet fish twenty years ago from Dicky, and now the legacy is passed on to you. A sharp, flexible fillet knife works well for the task, though you can do it with a smaller chef's knife, too. Make sure it's sharp.

Cut off the head at the back of the gills of the fish. Set it aside for the stockpot. Holding the fish by the tail, cut off the bottom fin.

With the fish lying on a cutting board, cut off the remaining fins. With your hand resting lightly on top of the fish, insert the knife point and make a "cheater cut" from the cavity (where the guts used to be) to the top of the tail. This makes it easier to cut the long fillet when you get there.

Next, angling your knife so that it rests on top of the backbone, insert your knife inside the fish and cut from head to tail, splitting the fish in half. Open the fish like a book.

Cut out the spine and save it for the stockpot.

Rotate the fish 180 degrees so that the head is now at your left hand. Using thin cuts nearly parallel to the board, cut out the rib or belly bones visible in the part of the salmon near the head. When you're cutting, you should always be able to see your knife through the flesh. If you can't, you're cutting off too much flesh with the bones. You now have a whole butterflied salmon. You could stuff that sucker with lemon slices and herbs and tie it shut, then

BOOK IT: BUTTERFLIED, BONED, AND OPENED UP LIKE A BOOK.

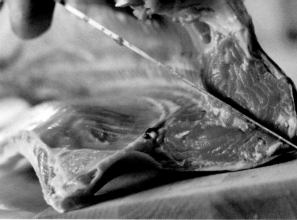

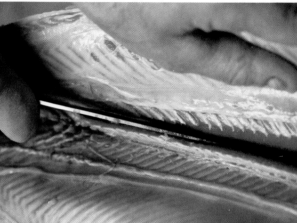

grill or roast it. Or you could separate the two fillets.

While you're working, remember these tips: keep the tip of your knife on the board for added control and always cut away from you. Also, the angle of the knife determines your fillet technique. Don't waste fish when you're removing the fillets, a practice that's maybe more art than science. And most of all, make like Rocky Balboa and stay loose. Let your knife do the work. If you start white-knuckling it and getting tense, your cuts will suffer.

CLEANING A MACKEREL

Our mackerel come to us whole and frozen, so they need to be cleaned before cooking. If you don't want to get your hands dirty, ask us to do it. If you're a self-starter, here you go. Warning: mackerel have sharp fins that easily cut you, as do many other fish, like rockfish. Be careful of their pokey bits when handling them.

Begin by cutting off the head or removing the gills if you'd like to keep the head on.

Insert the tip of the knife into the belly and run the knife along the belly from top to anus. Clean the fish under running water and pull out all the guts. You're done! If you like, at this point you can cut the fillet off each side.

DEVEINING A SHRIMP OR PRAWN

Your best friend here is a pair of kitchen scissors. We use ours for everything from cleaning sardines to snipping squid.

Holding the shrimp in one hand, the head pointed toward you, insert the tip of the scissors between the shell and the flesh on the back of the shrimp. Cut

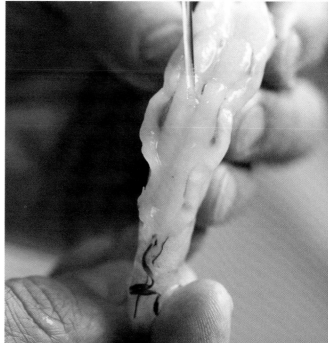

HOW TO THROW A BAG OF ROCKS

THE LOB

THE ONE-HANDED SET SHOT

THE SKYHOOK

THE OVER-THE-HEAD BLIND SHOT

BEHIND THE BACK AND OVER THE HEAD

UNDER THE LEG

Before you practice with whole fish, we recommend training with a good old-fashioned Bag o' Rocks, which is what we call a bag of clams when we're flinging them through the air. Especially if you're training for more complicated maneuvers like the under the leg (watch those fins) or the over-the-head blind shot. Makes a great alternative to Kettlebell training.

through the shell all the way down the back of the shrimp to the tail. You should see a black line, or the intestine, running along the length of the shrimp. Under cool running water, just pull and rub gently to remove the vein. You're done! If you like, while you have the shrimp under the running water, you can easily pull off the shell if that's required for your recipe. Save those shells for stock.

HOW TO SHUCK AN OYSTER

Before you begin shucking (which simply means opening up the oysters), you will need two things: a heavy-duty glove or a towel to protect your hand and an oyster knife. Oyster knives are cheap and perfectly suited for the task of prying open that shell, being thick and sturdy with the proper tip. It's worth it to buy an oyster knife for the task, even if you think it's a one-time deal; once you've shucked your own, we're sure you'll do it again. If you're serving the oysters on the half shell, have a large platter heaped with crushed ice ready so that you can place the shucked oysters immediately on the ice for a chill.

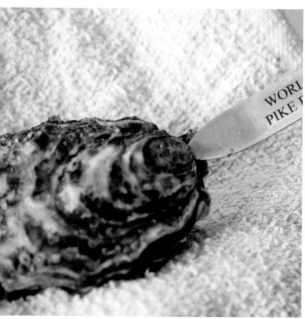

The directions that follow are for a right-handed person. If you're left-handed, flip the directions around.

Place a thick glove or oven mitt on your left hand, or hold a folded towel in your left hand on which you will place the oyster. The hinge (pointy side) should be sticking out and the cupped part of the oyster should be on the bottom. Oyster knives are sharp—don't make any mistake about that—and this will protect your hand if the knife slips. Having the cupped side down means you won't lose the juice or oyster liquor when you open the oyster up—that would be a crime. It's delicious.

Insert the tip of the oyster knife near the hinge, wiggling it a little if need be to get it in about one-half inch or so. It needs to go in only far enough to give you leverage to pry open the shell.

Holding the oyster firmly, slide the knife around the lip of the oyster until you reach the other side of the hinge. The oyster should remain level so you don't lose the liquid inside. Keep the knife inserted about one-half inch and the tip pointed slightly up.

Keeping the oyster level (save that juice!), pry the shell apart using the knife and/or your fingers. Before removing the top shell completely, use the oyster knife to cut any muscle that still clings to the inside of the top shell. Remove and discard the top shell.

Run the oyster knife under the oyster in the shell to detach the muscle holding it to the bottom shell. (There's nothing worse than tossing back an oyster on the half shell only to have it stick to the shell while the juice goes into your mouth!) For a nice half-shell presentation, flip over the oyster in its shell so it's nice and plump looking. Repeat with the remaining oysters.

CLEANING A DUNGENESS CRAB

Cleaning a crab isn't a difficult process, but it's messy. You'll want to clean the crab at the sink or with access to running water. Chill the crab quickly after cleaning. All the crabs we sell were cooked out at sea, and the instructions that follow are for a crab unable to reach out and pinch you.

HOW TO THROW A DUNGENESS CRAB

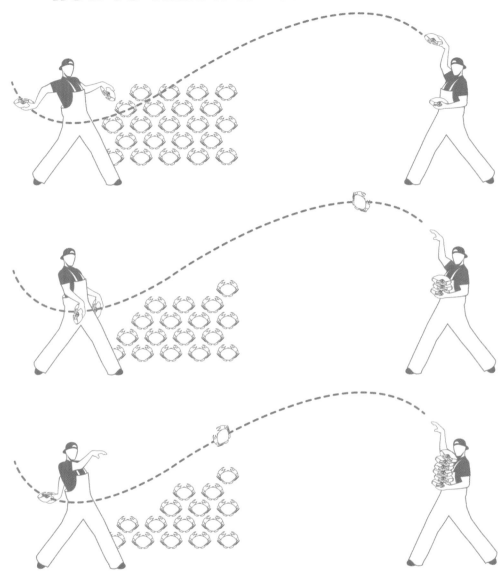

The toss 'n' stack combines the carefree nature of a salmon belly twist with balancing magic worthy of a circus performer on the receiving end. We find the flat nature of the crab's carapace adds critical stability here. Throw in a unicycle and it's practically a seafood-themed Cirque de Soleil.

Starting rule of thumb: never look a crab in the eye. What this means is that you always start with the back when you're cleaning a crab. If you've ever gone crabbing, you learned to recognize the "apron" on the bottom of a crab. It is wider and more oval on a female (which must be thrown back so it can make more crab babies) and slimmer on a male. Locate the apron on the bottom back of the crab, flip it up, and use your thumb to break it off and discard.

Stick your thumb into the hole where the apron used to be and gently pry off the carapace, or the crab's main shell. It should come off in one piece, maybe trailing some goo. Rinse and save that shell for the stockpot.

Next, look for the "dead man's fingers," a colorful but descriptive name for the crab's spongy gills. Rip them off and discard. Then, not to be indelicate, rip off the crab's face, or the mandibles at the front of the crab. Discard.

Under running water, flip the crab upside down, grip the legs on either side with your thumbs in the middle, and break the crab cleanly down the middle. It shouldn't take much effort. Some people really love to eat the goo you find inside. In general, we don't. We rinse the crab clean under the water.

That's it. Your crab's ready to be eaten. If you're just going to pick and eat the meat (one of the best ways to eat it), you may want to crack the claws lightly with a hammer or crab cracker. Even a butter knife works: grab the blade and smack the crab with the handle. The pointed tips of the smaller legs make lovely picks for getting meat out of tight spaces.

YOU'RE THROWING AWAY THE BEST PART

Of course we love it when you spend money buying fish, but part of sustainability is about avoiding waste. Just as there's more to a cow than filet mignon, there's more to fish than fillets. Learning how to use the bones, the heads, the collars, and other choice bits not only gives you great options for dinner, but extends your food dollar and does justice to a fish that was harvested to be used as food. If you ask any one of us, we'll tell you that some of those pieces you would never think to buy are the ones we prefer to take home to our families because they're full of flavor and richness.

Twenty years ago when he drove deliveries, longtime fishmonger Sam would go pick up whole tuna loins for us to sell. When he was at the distribution point, he noticed the bellies of all those tuna in the discard pile. Tuna belly! (At your favorite sushi bar, that belly is the richest, most expensive, and most sought after piece of fish in the joint.) He asked if he could take them home, and the fishermen were all too happy to oblige. Oh, was Sam a happy and well-fed man. Now, of course, people are on to the gig

MEET YOUR FISHMONGER

SAM SAMSON: YEARS AS A FISHMONGER: 26 FAVORITE SEAFOOD: MACKEREL

a bit more. You'd be hard pressed to find anyone tossing out tuna belly anymore, but there are plenty of people who still wouldn't look twice at a salmon collar. The collar is the bit between the gills and the first fin on the fish that connects the head and body. If you're Japanese, we're probably not telling you anything new, but take that beauty, sprinkle it with salt, and broil, and you have one of the tastiest parts of the fish.

Fishmonger Ryan was asked to speak at a food-centered event for artists, designers, architects, and chefs. As a topic, he decided to think small. In preparation for his talk, he watched our scraps and trimmings and noticed who was buying them. He asked the purchasers how they prepared them, then tracked and photographed the uses. In nice sushi restaurants, the collars and bellies (or *kama* and *toro*) of salmon, black cod, and tuna were

THRIFTY BONUS RECIPE: CRAB OIL

Simmer 1 to 2 pounds of crab shells, 2 to 4 cups of canola oil, a pinch of saffron threads, and 1 to 2 teaspoons of crushed red pepper flakes over low heat for several hours. Strain and store up to one week in the refrigerator. Crab oil can garnish bisque or étouffée, and it's great on fried eggs, too.

served to eager guests who loved the fatty qualities of the pieces. In small Asian restaurants, the salmon collars were used to make a sour fish soup called *sinigang* and other soups, stews, and noodle dishes. He went to markets around the International District in Seattle, where all manner of scraps and trimmings were being sold for good money, including salmon collars and halibut bellies, rockfish heads and bones. Even black cod bellies were going for thirty dollars a pound. After preparing for the event, he had a newfound appreciation of what was left over after a fish had been filleted. He started to take some of the ideas and incorporate them into his kitchen. (He even traded some salmon heads and tips for flowers for his girlfriend. Now that's smart.)

Today, his hands-down favorite fish recipe is to cut a giant collar with a substantial amount of fillet attached and roast it until the skin is crispy and brown. Just as butchers like to cut out and name their own special cuts, Ryan has coined the Royalty Cut, or a one-pound fillet attached to the collar. Food fit for a king!

TIPS FOR SCALE-TO-TAIL EATING

We're joking about the scale part. That really may be the only part of the fish we don't eat.

Save everything. With imagination and a little know-how you'll find a use.

Use a spoon to scrape bones and you'll get enough meat to make delicious fish cakes and salmon burgers.

Use your smoker to develop the oil and fats of collars and bellies into serious flavors.

Get out your stockpot. Take whitefish bones and heads and cook for fewer than thirty minutes to make fish stock that will add real flavor to your meal.

Save your shells. Crab, prawn, and lobster shells can be used to make stocks, infuse oils, and make bisques. They are loaded with flavor.

PART III

RECIPES

PREVIOUS PAGES: Anders, Ryan, Jake, and Sam in front of a Washington State ferry.
ABOVE: Under the famed clock of Pike Place Market.

SMOKIN', GRILLIN', AND CHILLIN'

THE FISHMONGER'S PANTRY

As a group we believe that with a well-equipped pantry and a pound of fish, you're minutes from an amazing meal. To spare you all our opinions, we narrowed them down to Ryan Rector's and Jake's suggestions for products you should always have on hand.

RECTOR'S REQUIREDS

Oil with a high smoke point (the temperature at which it burns) for getting a great sear on your fish. We like (and sell) avocado oil, which is also great for you, but grapeseed works, too.

Wondra is a superfine flour that is great for dredging. It creates a thin, crispy coating and you barely know it's there.

Lemons are a natural accompaniment to fish, cutting its oiliness.

Crushed red pepper flakes add a kick.

White wine carries flavor and creates a quick sauce or steaming liquid.

MEET YOUR FISHMONGER

JUSTIN HALL: YEARS AS A FISHMONGER: 25 FAVORITE SEAFOOD: KING SALMON

Kosher salt or sea salt heightens flavors.

Miso paste is made from fermented soybeans and has amazing salty depth.

Capers, like lemon, help cut a fish's richness.

Whole grain mustard can be used to emulsify oil and vinegar or to add a little spice.

JAKE'S JUST-GOT-TO-HAVE-ITS

Mixed peppercorns add color and flavor.

Fresh herbs, chopped at the last minute, bring loads of flavor.

Citrus, including orange and grapefruit, brightens a dish; lime is almost as necessary as air.

Champagne, red wine, and balsamic vinegars can bring sour or sweeter notes.

Toasted sesame oil adds a nutty richness with just a few drops.

Good extra-virgin olive oil is perfect for vinaigrettes, mixed with lemon and brushed on fish—you name it. Great extra-virgin oil is a sauce in itself.

Soy sauce adds salty depth and flavor.

Black bean sauce is great with whitefish or clams.

Pike Place Fish seasonings (see pages 242–248) are everything you need. Make up a bottle and keep on hand for instant flavor (or you can always buy them from us).

OPPOSITE: Justin making his justifiably famous Crab-Stuffed Morels (recipe page 99).

RISE AND SHINE

The sun is up, the coffee's brewing, and there's fish frying. It must be breakfast time. Take it from the crew, there is no better way to start the day. We're talking creamy quiche stuffed with crab and bell peppers, and bacon, of course. Had a little too much fun last night? We've got the cure for what ails you in the form of sautéed snapper dredged in our Cajun and Blackening Seasoning, just spicy enough to give you a jolt—served on a melting pillow of grits with some luscious avocado and juicy, ripe tomatoes on the side. An over-easy egg adds just the right touch.

Or maybe your mother-in-law is coming for brunch? No problem. Dungeness crab–topped eggs bake up on a bed of smoked salmon, all tucked into a fancy little toast cup. Or maybe a goat cheese–smoked salmon tart, with more cream and cheese than she, along with everyone else who asks for seconds, ever would admit to enjoying as much as she does. For those of you still skeptical about the seafood-breakfast combo, there's enough bacon in these recipes to put you in your comfort zone—before knocking your socks off. And there's always the Sunday-morning staple: toasted bagels with cream cheese, lox, capers, and red onions. Leave granola to the squirrels and wake up to some seafood.

DUNGENESS CRAB AND BACON QUICHE

If you're already thinking that a quiche is out of reach for you—what, make piecrust?—then let us change your mind. Combining the ease of a store-bought piecrust and the incredible deliciousness of Dungeness crab, this is a recipe that will land in your file of must-haves. Fishmonger Anders likes to top his slice with just a touch of hot sauce. Playing against the sweetness of the crabmeat and the richness of the bacon and the cheese, it's genius. If you're really pressed for time, you don't have to bake the shell before filling it, but the bottom may get a little soggy. Baking the shell beforehand makes for even slicing and a better texture.

MAKES ONE 9-INCH QUICHE

One 9-inch ready-made pie crust, chilled
1 teaspoon avocado oil or unsalted butter
½ cup diced red bell pepper
½ cup diced mushrooms
½ cup chopped spinach
½ pound Dungeness crabmeat, picked over
4 bacon slices, cooked and crumbled
½ cup shredded Swiss cheese
¼ cup shredded Parmesan cheese
4 large eggs
1½ cups half-and-half
Kosher salt and freshly ground black pepper
Few pinches ground nutmeg
Few pinches cayenne pepper
Bottled hot sauce (optional)

Preheat the oven to 400°F.

Remove the piecrust from the refrigerator. If the crust is not in its own aluminum container, use the dough to line a pie plate, trimming the edges as

MEET YOUR FISHMONGER
CHARLIE TRIMARCO: YEARS AS A FISHMONGER: 1 FAVORITE SEAFOOD: SNOOK (A SALTWATER FISH PLENTIFUL IN FLORIDA)

needed. If the dough warms up while you are working with it, put it back into the fridge to chill before continuing.

Using a fork, poke the crust in several places along the bottom and on the sides. This keeps the crust from ballooning up as it bakes (and you need to save room for all that delicious crab you're going to stuff inside).

Line the dough with a piece of parchment paper or aluminum foil and then fill the shell one-half to two-thirds full with metal pie weights or dried beans or rice. (You shouldn't cook with the beans or rice after using them as pie weights, so make sure you put them aside in a special container when you're through. You can reuse them as pie weights again and again.) The weights work to keep the shell's shape while baking.

Bake the crust for about 10 minutes, or just until the edges look dry and firm. Remove from the oven, then remove the weights and parchment paper. Set aside.

Turn down the oven to 375°F.

While you're prebaking the crust, cook the filling. Heat the avocado oil in a sauté pan over medium-high heat. Add the bell pepper and mushrooms and sauté for 2 to 3 minutes. Add the chopped spinach and sauté for about 1 minute, or until the spinach starts to wilt. Remove from the heat and place the mixture in a large bowl.

Add the crabmeat, bacon, half of the Swiss cheese, and all the Parmesan to the bowl with the vegetables. Stir gently to mix. In a separate bowl, lightly beat the eggs. Add the half-and-half to the eggs and season with salt and black pepper. Add the nutmeg and cayenne.

Spread the crabmeat mixture evenly over the bottom of the prebaked piecrust. Pour the egg mixture into the crust until it is ¼ inch from the top. Sprinkle the remaining Swiss cheese evenly over the filling. Place the quiche on the middle rack of the oven and bake for 45 minutes, or until golden brown. Test for doneness by sticking a toothpick into the center. It should come out clean.

Remove the quiche to a cooling rack and let sit for 5 to 10 minutes. Slice and enjoy. Serve with hot sauce, if desired.

GRITS AND GRUNTS

Grunts are a fish you'll probably never see on a menu and will most definitely never see at a fish market, especially on the West Coast. But as Charlie knows, they inhabit every dock, marina, pier, reef, and any other underwater structure in southern Florida. Because they are considered vastly inferior in taste to their snapper relatives, they're targeted for quick and easy meals by the fishermen in the Florida Keys, where this breakfast dish originates.

Considering grunt is largely unavailable (and truthfully, Charlie says, isn't very good), here we substitute small fillets of snapper or rockfish. This is an incredible dish—full of rich and spicy flavors, with a wild array of textures, from the pillow of creamy grits to searing fish to the crisp bacon. The classic accompaniment to grits and grunts is cheap beer, but coffee works, too.

SERVES 2

Grits

5 cups water

1 teaspoon kosher salt, plus more to taste

1 cup instant grits

2 tablespoons (¼ stick) unsalted butter

3 bacon slices, diced

½ sweet onion, diced, such as Walla Walla

4 snapper or rockfish fillets

4 to 6 tablespoons Cajun and Blackening Seasoning (page 247)

Kosher salt and freshly ground black pepper

3 tablespoons unsalted butter

2 large eggs

1 avocado, peeled, pitted, and sliced

1 tomato, sliced

First, prepare the grits. Bring the water and salt to a boil in a heavy-bottomed pot. Whisking the whole time, add the grits in a steady stream.

Reduce the heat to low or medium-low and cook, stirring frequently, for 10 minutes, or until the grits have bloomed and are creamy. Stir in the butter and taste for salt. Keep warm.

Fry the bacon in a large sauté pan over medium heat, until crispy. Remove the bacon to paper towels to drain. Add the onion to the pan and sauté in the bacon fat until soft. Keep warm.

Coat the fillets thoroughly with Cajun seasoning and sprinkle both sides with salt and pepper. Heat the butter in a large clean sauté pan or in the bacon pan over medium-high heat. Add the fish fillets and fry for 2 to 3 minutes per side, or until just cooked through. While the fish is cooking, crack the eggs into the pan and fry alongside the fish, or fry in a separate skillet if the pan is not large enough to accommodate both.

Spoon the grits into two large shallow serving bowls and sprinkle with the bacon and sautéed onion. Top each with 2 fish fillets and crown with an egg. Lay the sliced avocado and tomato on the side and season with salt and pepper.

CRAB AND ASPARAGUS SCRAMBLE

Here's a recipe that celebrates spring—and that's cause for celebration in rainy Seattle—a time when the sun starts to poke out a bit and green things have just started appearing in the market. This crab scramble is at once simple enough for a basic weekend morning and good enough for company brunch. Make sure you gently squeeze any extra moisture from the crabmeat before adding it to the scramble to keep the scramble creamy.

SERVES 2

8 to 10 medium asparagus spears

½ cup Dungeness crabmeat, picked over

4 large eggs

2 tablespoons heavy cream

Kosher salt and freshly ground black pepper

2 tablespoons (¼ stick) unsalted butter

2 tablespoons chopped fresh chives

Trim the tough ends from the asparagus by bending each spear until it snaps at its natural breaking point. Discard the ends and thinly slice each stalk on the diagonal. Leave the tips whole. Set aside.

Drain the excess liquid from the crabmeat by setting it in a strainer and gently squeezing the moisture out with a paper towel. Separate the crab with your fingers and set aside.

Using a fork or whisk, beat together the eggs and cream in a medium bowl. Season with salt and pepper.

Heat a heavy-bottomed pan over medium heat. Melt the butter and add the asparagus. Cook, stirring frequently, for 1 to 2 minutes, or until the asparagus brightens in color. Don't overcook. Add the egg mixture and swirl in the pan. Sprinkle over the crabmeat and gently fold together until the eggs are set. The mixture should be creamy but not runny. Add salt and pepper to taste. Sprinkle with chives and serve immediately.

EGGS IN A BASKET

Because of its name, we find these Ryan Yokoyama specials are particularly suited for Easter brunch, but quick enough that you can make them anytime for a fun treat. In order to achieve perfect baskets, you must use ordinary white sandwich bread. Yes, the squishy kind with no nutritional value loved by kids (and fishmongers) everywhere.

SERVES 6

6 slices white sandwich bread

2 tablespoons (¼ stick) unsalted butter, melted

½ cup flaked smoked salmon

6 large eggs

Kosher salt and freshly ground black pepper

6 tablespoons heavy cream

¼ pound Dungeness crabmeat, picked over

Preheat the oven to 375°F. Butter 6 muffin cups.

Using a rolling pin, flatten each piece of bread to no more than ⅛ inch thick. Brush 1 bread slice with melted butter. Use the bread to line a muffin cup. Place it, buttered side down, in the cup, gently pushing down and out to the sides to mold the bread to the cup. Repeat with the remaining bread slices. Bake the bread cups until the bread crisps, 3 to 5 minutes. Remove from the oven.

Divide the smoked salmon among the bottoms of the toast cups. Crack an egg into each cup. Season with salt and pepper. Top each egg with 1 tablespoon of the heavy cream. Bake until the whites are just set, 10 to 14 minutes. Top each egg with crabmeat and serve immediately.

CROQUE MADAME WITH LOX

Here we are getting all fancy and French on you. For those who don't know, a *croque madame* (please say it with the proper accent) is a classic French bistro staple that's really nothing more than a grilled ham and cheese sandwich with cheese sauce on the top as well as an egg. We swapped out the ham for silky lox and put all the cheese in the sauce. This is rich, very rich (did someone say bacon fat?), but very good. Change it up and try serving it as a light supper dish with a salad on a cold fall evening.

SERVES 2

3 bacon strips
2 tablespoons all-purpose flour
1 cup whole milk
¼ cup grated sharp white cheddar cheese
2 tablespoons shredded Parmesan cheese
4 slices sourdough bread
1 tablespoon unsalted butter
2 large eggs
Kosher salt and freshly ground black pepper
8 thin slices lox

Dice the bacon and place in a cold sauté pan. Slowly cook the bacon over low heat until the fat is rendered and the bacon is crisp. Remove the bacon to a plate lined with paper towels.

Measure 2 tablespoons of bacon fat and place in a clean saucepan over medium heat. Add the flour and whisk constantly for 2 to 3 minutes, to remove the floury taste. Add the milk in a steady stream, whisking constantly to avoid lumps. Add the cheddar and Parmesan and whisk until the cheese melts. Keep warm.

Toast the bread. Heat the butter in a frying pan over medium heat. Add the eggs and fry until set. Season with salt and pepper.

Place a piece of toast on each of two plates. Top each with 4 slices of lox, then another slice of toast. Spoon some cheese sauce on top of each sandwich and sprinkle with some bacon. Place 1 egg on top of each sandwich. Serve immediately.

SMOKED SALMON AND GOAT CHEESE TART

There's just something right about smoked salmon and goat cheese—the richness of the fish is offset nicely by the salty tang of the cheese. We'd be lying if we said this was light, though. The cream and the Gruyère won't do anything for your gut, but boy, they taste good. If you don't have pie weights to line the tart dough when prebaking the crust, you can use raw beans or rice. Make sure you line the dough before dumping them in, or you'll be picking beans out of your puff pastry.

SERVES 6 TO 8

1 sheet puff pastry

6 large eggs

1½ cups heavy cream

4 ounces Gruyère, Emmenthaler, or other Swiss-type cheese

6 ounces smoked salmon

1 ounce firm goat cheese

Preheat the oven to 375°F.

Unfold the puff pastry and lay it in a 10½-inch pie plate or tart pan. Trim the pastry to fit, pressing the edges into the sides of the pan. Prick the bottom of the crust generously with a fork to keep the bottom flat while baking. Line the crust with aluminum foil or parchment paper and fill with pie weights (or raw beans or rice). Bake for 20 minutes. Remove from the oven, remove the foil and pie weights, and return the crust to the oven for 15 minutes, or until lightly golden.

While the crust is baking, whisk together the eggs and cream in a medium bowl. Grate the Gruyère into another bowl and set aside.

When the crust is ready, remove from the oven. Sprinkle the Gruyère into the bottom of the crust. Flake the smoked salmon with your fingers and add it to the crust. Crumble the goat cheese with your fingers and distribute it evenly over the salmon. Pour in the egg mixture to cover.

Return the tart to the oven for 30 minutes and bake until firm. If the crust becomes too brown during baking, cover the crust only with strips of aluminum foil. To test if the tart is done, slide a knife into the center. If the knife comes out clean, the tart is ready. Cool for 10 minutes before serving.

LET'S GET THIS PARTY STARTED

How-*dee!* **This is the chapter where two of our favorite aspects of** seafood cooking come to the forefront. Number one: seafood is celebratory. (While we might be around fish quite a bit, most everyone else thinks of seafood as celebration food.) So, when you start off a meal with a seafood appetizer, whether there are four of you or forty, you've already set a festive mood. Number two: seafood is fast. There are more important things to think about when you're having a party or having people over for dinner. Who wants to be stuck in the kitchen for hours so that by the time people arrive you're too tired to enjoy yourself? With seafood apps there's no need, because you can whip up something fabulous in less time than it takes to chill your beer.

Think tongue-tingling Thai curry mussels or quick-sautéed squid bathed in so much butter and garlic you want to dive in and swim around in the bowl. Go fancy with a suave poached and smoked salmon spread or low country with BBQ shrimp. Or get crabby: stuff sweet Dungeness crab into morel mushrooms, mix crab with shrimp and form it into cakes, or make Dicky's justifiably famous crab dip. Make one, make them all, and get ready for a good time.

PROSCIUTTO-WRAPPED PRAWNS

The hardest part of this dish is wrapping the prawns in prosciutto, which is to say, it's a snap. Get the kids in on the action and you're home free! Perfect for a party, this recipe comes from Dan Bugge of Matt's in the Market, Pike Place Fish's beloved neighbor and customer (and did we also mention that Dan used to be one of the crew?).

SERVES 4 TO 6

1 pound thinly sliced prosciutto

2½ pounds large prawns, peeled and deveined

1 cup dry white wine

4 tablespoons (½ stick) unsalted butter

6 garlic cloves, finely chopped

3 fresh thyme sprigs

3 fresh marjoram sprigs

Wrap 1 slice of prosciutto like a blanket around each prawn.

Pour in enough white wine to cover the bottom of a large sauté pan, and bring to a boil over high heat. Reduce the heat to medium and add the butter, garlic, thyme, and marjoram.

Once the butter is melted, arrange the prawns in a single layer in the pan. (Using a circular pattern helps them fit.) Cook the prawns for 1½ to 2 minutes per side, or until each side is slightly firm and pink.

To serve, arrange the prawns on a large platter. Drizzle some of the cooking liquid over the top.

COLD MARINATED PENN COVE MUSSELS

Though most of us are accustomed to eating mussels hot, steamed in white wine or tossed with pasta, in lots of cultures mussels are enjoyed cold, sometimes stuffed and other times marinated, as are these lovely Penn Cove beauties here. This is a great make-ahead appetizer to enjoy with drinks. Penn Cove mussels come without "beards." If you are using a different type of mussel, grab the threads hanging out and pull toward the hinge of the mussel. With a sharp tug, the beard should come off.

SERVES 6 TO 8

3 pounds Penn Cove mussels, rinsed

1 quart cider vinegar

1¼ cups sugar

1 tablespoon finely chopped garlic

½ cup red onion slices

½ cup chopped green onions

Place the mussels in a large heavy pot with a lid. Place over high heat and cook, shaking the pot occasionally, until the mussels have opened, 5 to 6 minutes. Remove the mussels (in their shells) to a large bowl. Cover and place in the refrigerator to chill for at least 30 minutes.

Combine the vinegar, sugar, and garlic in a medium saucepan, and place over low heat. Cook, stirring, just until the sugar dissolves. Add the red onion and green onions and allow the marinade to cool slightly.

Pour the marinade over the mussels and stir to coat. Allow to marinate, covered, for at least 1 hour or even overnight to allow the flavors to blend.

OPPOSITE: Sam working on the line sorting mussels.

SALMON RILLETTES ON CROUSTADE

There is nothing wrong with the ubiquitous cream cheese–smoked salmon dip, surrounded by a ring of buttery crackers, that appears on the buffet table at every gathering. Okay, there *was* nothing wrong with it until we tasted salmon rillettes. The recipe uses both smoked salmon and poached salmon for a lighter touch and more balanced flavors than that old standby.

Throw out the fancy French name to impress your guests if you want, but rest assured that this salmon spread, from Seattle's Café Campagne in Pike Place Market, is easy to put together and a guaranteed hit at your next party. We literally can't stop eating it every time we make it, plus it can be made up to one day ahead of time and chilled until you're ready to serve. The poaching liquid recipe is a keeper on its own. Use it to poach fish for a light lunch.

MAKES 25

Croustade
1 baguette
Extra-virgin olive oil
Sea salt

Poached Salmon
¾ pound skinless, boneless wild salmon, cut into 1-inch pieces
2 quarts water
1 cup dry white wine
¼ cup white wine vinegar
1 carrot, thinly sliced
1 small onion or leek, thinly sliced
1 bay leaf
4 fresh parsley stems
½ teaspoon black peppercorns

½ cup mayonnaise
2 garlic cloves, finely minced

Juice of ½ lemon

2 cups poached salmon (from above)

½ pound smoked salmon, skin and bones removed

¼ cup capers, rinsed and drained

½ cup finely diced sweet onion, such as Walla Walla

2 tablespoons chopped fresh parsley

Sea salt and freshly ground black pepper

Preheat the oven to 400°F.

To make the croustade, slice the baguette into ⅓-inch pieces and place in a bowl. Drizzle a little olive oil over the slices and sprinkle with salt. Toss well to coat. Lay the baguette slices out on a sheet pan. Bake for 5 to 7 minutes, or until lightly browned and crisp. Remove to a plate to cool.

To poach the salmon, place the salmon pieces in a shallow baking pan. In a medium saucepan, bring the water, white wine, vinegar, carrot, onion, bay leaf, parsley stems, and peppercorns to a boil over high heat. Lower the heat and simmer for 10 minutes. Pour the hot liquid through a strainer over the salmon. Allow the salmon to poach for 5 minutes, or until just opaque. Remove the salmon to a bowl and set aside to cool. Discard the poaching liquid.

Whisk together the mayonnaise, garlic, and lemon juice in a medium bowl, until smooth. Add the poached salmon, smoked salmon, capers, onion, and parsley and fold gently with a spatula. It is not necessary to shred the poached salmon. The mixing action should be sufficient to break down the fish to about ½-inch pieces. Adjust the seasoning with salt, fresh pepper, and additional lemon juice to taste.

Serve the rillettes spread on the croustade or in a bowl surrounded by croustade. If the salmon spread is made ahead and chilled, allow to come to room temperature before serving.

GRANDPA CZERWONKA'S BBQ SHRIMP

Though we've never met the man, we wish we could eat shrimp with our friend Jennifer's grandpa and thank him for coming up with a recipe this good. Start with great shrimp and you're halfway there. Add spiced butter and bacon? Forget about it. You'll need napkins or, better yet, just lick your fingers.

SERVES 8

½-pound (2 sticks) unsalted butter

2 cups chicken broth

2 tablespoons Dijon mustard

1½ teaspoons chili powder

¼ teaspoon dried basil

¼ teaspoon dried thyme

2 teaspoons freshly ground black pepper

½ teaspoon dried oregano

2 garlic cloves, minced

2 tablespoons minced yellow onion

1 tablespoon Cajun and Blackening Seasoning (page 247) or Northwest
  Seafood Seasoning (page 242)

½ pound bacon, diced and cooked until crispy

2 to 3 pounds large shrimp, shells on, split down the back and deveined

Preheat the oven to 400°F.

Heat the butter in a large saucepan over medium heat. Add the chicken broth, mustard, chili powder, basil, thyme, pepper, oregano, garlic, onion, Cajun seasoning, and bacon. Over low heat, simmer briefly to combine the flavors, whisking occasionally.

Place the shrimp in a 13 x 9-inch baking dish and pour the sauce mixture over the shrimp. Bake for 15 to 20 minutes, or until the shrimp are opaque. Transfer shrimp and sauce to a deep platter or bowl to serve. Offer bread for dipping into the sauce.

RYAN'S CRAB QUESADILLA

Though we don't always advocate putting a lot of cheese with your seafood, crab seems to take to cheese like a fish to water. This easy and delicious appetizer is a hit with kids if you watch the crushed red pepper flakes. Your buddies would also be very happy if you served this to them while you are watching a game. Or, they may never leave. The risk is yours.

SERVES 4

1 cup chopped onions
Kosher salt and freshly ground pepper
Crushed red pepper flakes
1 pound crabmeat, picked over
2 tablespoons fresh lime juice
Handful fresh cilantro, chopped
8 flour tortillas
8 ounces pepper Jack cheese, shredded

Heat a nonstick skillet over medium heat. Sauté the onions with a pinch of salt, pepper, and red pepper flakes to taste. When the onions are soft, transfer to a bowl. Add the crabmeat, lime juice, and cilantro. Mix to combine.

Wipe out the skillet and place over medium heat. Place a tortilla in the hot pan and layer with some of the cheese, crabmeat mixture, and more cheese. Top with another tortilla. Cook until the tortilla is slightly brown and crispy, then flip it. Once the other side is crispy, remove from the pan and cut into triangles. Repeat with the remaining tortillas, cheese, and crab mixture.

SHRIMP AND CRAB CAKES

We could give you a surefire recipe for crab cakes. (In fact, we do: see the variation below.) But we found that incorporating shrimp into a crab cake does nothing to diminish the rich flavor of the crab and adds excellent texture to boot. It also doesn't hurt that, on the whole, shrimp are a heck of a lot more affordable than Dungeness crabs, giving you more value for your money. Serve with a tartar or even an Asian-inspired sauce; place on a split English muffin and drizzle with hollandaise for brunch; or make tiny cakes and set them out as appetizers. No matter how you serve them, these cakes are winners.

MAKES 12

Extra-virgin olive oil

½ shallot, minced

2 celery stalks, finely diced

2 jalapeño or serrano chiles, diced (optional), or ½ small green bell
   pepper, stemmed, seeded, and cut into small dice

1 tablespoon fresh thyme, chopped

2 pounds shrimp, peeled, deveined, and chopped

Zest of ½ lemon, plus juice of 1 lemon

2 tablespoons chopped fresh parsley

1 tablespoon chopped fresh chives

1 tablespoon chopped fresh dill

¼ cup mayonnaise

6 ounces Dungeness crabmeat, picked

1½ cups fresh bread crumbs

Kosher salt and freshly ground black pepper

2 large eggs, lightly beaten

All-purpose flour, for dredging

Unsalted butter and extra-virgin olive oil

Heat 1 to 2 tablespoons of olive oil in a medium sauté pan, over medium-high heat. Add the shallot, celery, chiles, and thyme and sauté until the vegetables are limp but not brown. Add the shrimp and sauté until just cooked through. Transfer to a glass bowl and allow to cool slightly, 10 to 15 minutes.

In the bowl with the cooled shrimp mixture, combine the lemon zest, juice, parsley, chives, and dill and mix well. Add the mayonnaise, crabmeat, and bread crumbs. Taste for salt and pepper. Add the eggs and mix gently to combine, making sure not to break up the crabmeat too much. Cover the bowl and refrigerate for at least 1 hour or up to 3.

Divide the mixture into 12 portions and pat into cakes about 3 inches in diameter. Mix flour with salt and pepper in a shallow bowl, then dredge the cakes on both sides. Place a large sauté pan over medium heat and add equal amounts of butter and olive oil. Fry the shrimp and crab cakes until golden brown and heated through, 3 to 4 minutes on each side.

VARIATION: If you want to go the traditional route, omit the shrimp and increase the crabmeat to a scant ¾ pound (the meat from about 1½ Dungeness crabs). Decrease the mayonnaise to 2 tablespoons.

THAI CURRY MUSSELS

Impress your guests with this easy starter from **Penn Cove Shellfish**, made easy with store-bought Thai curry paste accented with more ginger, some coconut, and lime. A nice change of pace for those who love clams, petite Penn Cove mussels are sustainably farmed off the coast of Whidbey Island near Seattle, and are sought after for their sweet, tender flesh.

Make sure you use coconut "water" or juice, not coconut milk, for the dish. Coconut water is the liquid collected from the interior of young coconuts and has a much lighter body and fresher taste than coconut milk. You can find it at Asian markets and many larger supermarkets.

Warning: There is some spice to this dish. If you want to dial down the heat, use less Thai curry paste, or remove the seeds and ribs from the chile, or eliminate the chile altogether. Add some crusty bread for dunking and enjoy with white wine or beer.

SERVES 4

1 cup dry sake

1 cup coconut water

1 tablespoon Thai red curry paste

1 tablespoon Hungarian paprika

1 tablespoon yellow curry powder

1 jalapeño or serrano chile, deribbed and minced

2 limes

1 pound Penn Cove mussels, debearded* and rinsed

2 Roma tomatoes, chopped

2 green onions, finely chopped

2 garlic cloves, thinly sliced

1 tablespoon minced fresh ginger

Penn Cove mussels do not need to be debearded. If you are using another type of mussel, grab hold of the threads near the base—the "beard"—and pull toward the tip of the mussel with a sharp tug. The beard should break off cleanly.

Thai curry mussels provided by Penn Cover Shellfish.

Kosher salt

⅓ cup chopped fresh cilantro

Combine the sake, coconut water, red curry paste, paprika, curry powder, and jalapeño in a large heavy pot or Dutch oven with a lid. Whisk thoroughly and place over high heat. Using a Microplane or small box grater, remove the zest of 1 of the limes and add to the pot. Juice both limes and add to the mixture, stirring to combine. Bring to a boil over high heat.

Add the mussels to the pot and cover. Cook until the mussels just open, 3 to 4 minutes. Using a slotted spoon, transfer the mussels to a large shallow bowl, discarding any mussels that remain closed. Cover the mussels to keep warm.

Add half of the chopped tomatoes, the green onions, garlic, and ginger to the pot and simmer until the garlic is tender, stirring occasionally, about 4 minutes. Season with salt.

Pour the liquid over the mussels. Garnish with the remaining tomatoes and the cilantro and serve immediately.

LEMON PEPPER CLAMS WITH BREAD CRUMBS

Finally, a recipe that uses black pepper as less of a given and more of the bracing, kicky spice that it is. There's *a lot* of pepper in here—enough to give it real heat—but it's offset so nicely by the lemon and the richness of bacon. When we tested this recipe from Seattle's Steelhead Diner, we found ourselves going back, and back, and back again to dip another clam out of the bowl until the clams were *gone.* They were that good. Pernod is an anise-flavored liquor that adds nice depth. You don't taste it per se, but you'll notice if you leave it out.

SERVES 6 TO 8 AS AN APPETIZER OR 4 FOR DINNER

Lemon Bread Crumbs
Zest of 3 lemons, chopped finely

½ cup dried bread crumbs

2 tablespoons chopped fresh parsley

¼ cup extra-virgin olive oil

¼ pound bacon, diced

2 tablespoons extra-virgin olive oil

¼ cup finely diced celery

¼ cup finely diced carrot

¼ cup finely diced onion

½ cup finely diced fennel bulb

1 tablespoon chopped garlic

3 tablespoons freshly ground black pepper

2 pounds Manila clams, washed well

3 tablespoons unsalted butter

¼ cup fresh lemon juice

¼ cup Pernod

To make the bread crumbs, first reserve half of the lemon zest. Then combine the remaining lemon zest, the bread crumbs, parsley, and olive oil in a mixing bowl and set aside.

Cook the bacon in a large heavy-bottomed pot over medium heat until crisp and the fat is rendered, 8 to 10 minutes. Remove the bacon to paper towels to drain. Pour off the fat and reserve.

Heat the olive oil in the same pot over medium heat. Add the celery, carrot, onion, and fennel and cook until tender. Add the garlic and cook until fragrant. Stir in the pepper, then add the clams, butter, salt to taste, lemon juice, and Pernod. Sprinkle with bacon and the reserved zest and cover with a tight-fitting lid.

Cook until all the clams are open. Transfer them with a slotted spoon to a warmed platter. Reduce the remaining liquid by half over high heat. Taste the broth and adjust the seasoning. Finally, ladle the vegetable mixture, bacon, and broth over the clams and sprinkle with the lemon bread crumbs, trying to get a bit inside each clam.

DICKY'S AMAZING CRAB DIP

This tried-and-true favorite comes from Dicky Yokoyama, brother of Johnny, the owner of Pike Place Fish. Dicky's version starts with a can of cream of celery soup, but because the dip is so easy, we take it up a notch by making our own creamy base from scratch. The dip needs at least 3 hours in the refrigerator to set. Try to channel your inner planner. Letting the dip sit overnight is even better.

SERVES 10

2½ cups chicken broth

3 celery stalks, finely diced

1 carrot, finely diced

1 medium onion, diced

1½ cups heavy cream

2 tablespoons (¼ stick) unsalted butter

1½ teaspoons kosher salt, plus more to taste

½ teaspoon white pepper

Two 8-ounce packages cream cheese, softened

1 pound fresh crabmeat, flaked

1 cup mayonnaise

4 green onions, finely chopped, plus more for garnish

Crackers, vegetables, or chips, for serving

Bring the chicken broth to a boil in a medium saucepan over high heat. Add the celery, carrot, and onion. Reduce the heat and let simmer for 30 minutes. Allow to cool slightly. Add the cream and butter. Using a wand or stick blender, puree the mixture. Add the salt and white pepper and stir in the cream cheese. Chill until cold.

Stir in the crabmeat, mayonnaise, and green onions. Check the seasonings and add more salt to taste. Pour the dip into a shallow bowl or gratin dish. Cover and allow to set for at least 3 hours or overnight in the refrigerator. Sprinkle over a few green onions before serving with crackers, fresh vegetables, or chips.

CALAMARI PERSILLADE

Even though we probably mangle the pronunciation, we do know the term "persillade" simply means you should expect both garlic and parsley to show up in a dish. This is a move we always heartily endorse, and in this appetizer from our Market neighbor Café Campagne, the combination totally works. If you buy cleaned squid (calamari) from your fishmonger, this recipe takes five minutes to prepare. In fact, it goes so quickly that you should have everything ready to go before you start cooking. Make sure you have good bread on hand to sop up all that garlicky goodness at the bottom of the bowl.

SERVES 4

1 lemon
½ cup extra-virgin olive oil
¼ cup capers, drained and patted dry
1 pound squid, cleaned and cut into thin rings
⅓ cup peeled garlic cloves, finely chopped
¼ cup finely chopped fresh parsley
Kosher salt and freshly ground black pepper

Cut the lemon in half, then cut one half in wedges. Reserve.

Heat the olive oil in a sauté pan over high heat. Add the capers and cook, shaking the pan, until the capers begin to pop. Add calamari, garlic, and parsley and cook, stirring, just until the calamari begin to firm up and turn white (this should not take more than 1 minute). Squeeze the half lemon and add lemon juice to taste. Season with salt and plenty of pepper. Turn out the calamari into a warmed shallow bowl and serve with lemon wedges.

FRIES WITH EYES

Appearing in markets either fresh or frozen, smelt are various species of tiny little fish that spawn in rivers and make their way out to sea, much like salmon. Also like salmon, smelt are rich in good-for-you oils, have fantastic flavor, and are the easiest fish in the world to prepare. Why? Because you can follow the brilliant lead of the Seattle restaurant Madison Park Conservatory and fry them up, fins and skin and backbones intact. You cook them with heads on—hence "fries with eyes"—and eat them nose to tail. Dipped in a caper-and-dill–laced tartar sauce, "sustainable" has never tasted so good.

SERVES 4

Tartar Sauce
2 cups mayonnaise
½ cup chopped capers
1 tablespoon chopped shallot
1 tablespoon chopped fresh dill
Zest and juice of 1 lemon
1 teaspoon smoked paprika
1 teaspoon red wine vinegar
Kosher salt

Canola or peanut oil, for deep-frying
24 smelt, thawed, if frozen
2 cups all-purpose flour
Kosher salt and freshly cracked black pepper

To make the tartar sauce, combine the mayonnaise, capers, shallot, dill, lemon zest, lemon juice, paprika, vinegar, and a pinch of salt in a medium bowl. Whisk to combine. Taste for seasoning and adjust salt as desired. Set aside.

In a large heavy-bottomed pot, heat 2 to 3 inches canola oil to 375°F on a deep-fry thermometer.

"Fries with Eyes" provided by Madison Park Conservatory.

Using kitchen scissors, snip each smelt just across the gill cover, leaving the head attached. Next, snip each fish up the belly, starting at the tail end and cutting toward the first cut you made. Grasping the head, you should be able to grab and pull out the viscera. Rinse each fish under running water and pat dry.

Place the flour in a shallow bowl and season with plenty of salt and pepper. Dredge the fish in the seasoned flour, knocking off any excess. Fry in the hot oil until golden, 2 to 3 minutes, then remove to paper towels or crumpled brown paper to drain. Sprinkle with salt while hot and serve at once with the tartar sauce for dipping.

SILVER SMELT TATSUTA AGE

Here are smelt Japanese style, the way they do them at Seattle restaurant Sushi Kappo Tamura. The flavors are delicate but definitely there—the soy, ginger, and garlic. Using potato starch instead of flour keeps the smelt superlight.

SERVES 4

24 fresh silver smelt
¼ cup soy sauce
¼ cup sake or dry white wine
1 teaspoon grated fresh ginger
1 teaspoon minced garlic
Peanut oil, for frying
1½ cups potato starch
Lemon wedges
Hot sauce (optional)

Using kitchen scissors, snip each smelt just across the gill cover, leaving the head attached. Next, snip each fish up the belly, starting at the tail end and cutting toward the first cut you made. Grasping the head, you should be able to grab and pull out the viscera. Rinse each fish under running water and pat dry.

Combine the soy sauce, sake, ginger, and garlic in a medium bowl. Add the smelt and marinate for 10 minutes, then drain in a colander.

In a large heavy-bottomed pot, heat 2 to 3 inches peanut oil to 350°F on a deep-fry thermometer.

Place the potato starch in a shallow bowl. Dredge the fish, shaking off any excess.

Fry a few fish at a time to golden brown, 2 to 3 minutes. Drain briefly on paper towels. Serve with lemon wedges and hot sauce, if desired.

CRAB-STUFFED MORELS

Okay, so it's true how much it rains in Seattle. But do you know what? Rain makes our forests lush and makes delectable mushrooms pop up out of the forest floor like gangbusters. Justin likes to take beautiful morel mushrooms and pack them with crab and cheese and other good stuff and sear them just until hot and melty. Watch out, you'll want to start eating them before they're cool enough to handle.

MAKES 8 TO 10

8 to 10 large morel mushrooms, brushed
   clean
¼ pound Dungeness crabmeat, picked
   over
¼ cup finely grated Parmesan cheese
2 tablespoons minced garlic
3 tablespoons minced shallot
Kosher salt and freshly ground black
   pepper
Unsalted butter or butter and extra-virgin
   olive oil, for frying

Remove the stems from the morels. Discard or save them for another purpose.

Combine the crabmeat, Parmesan, garlic, and shallot in a small bowl and season with salt and pepper. Tightly pack the depression in the bottom of each morel (left by removing the stem) with some of the crab mixture.

Heat a couple of tablespoons of butter or a combination of butter and olive oil in a sauté pan over medium-high heat. Sauté, turning frequently, until all sides are seared, turning gently so that too much filling doesn't spill out. Cover the pan and allow the mushrooms to steam for 2 minutes. Serve at once.

SALMON

We smoke 'em, we throw 'em, we eat 'em. You guessed it: salmon. For all of us here in the Pacific Northwest, there is perhaps no more iconic (or delicious) fish. And for good reason. Pacific salmon have incomparable flavor and are rich in heart-loving omega-3s that also keep the fish moist when the fish are dried or smoked. Thousands of years ago, the native peoples from California to British Columbia to Alaska fished the waters for salmon that they ate fresh, dried, smoked, and roasted over wooden frames angled toward wood fires. (Maybe they even threw them—do you know they didn't?) Salmon were even used as currency and considered a form of wealth.

When Europeans moved to the West Coast and discovered the rich salmon runs, it appeared as if there was no end to this magnificent treasure. Now, of course, we know how tragically untrue this is. Even as far back as 1875, the first-ever fish commissioner reported that salmon stocks were in peril. But our habits didn't change; if anything, we doubled down on our pursuit of salmon. Various factors, from the loss of marshland along our own Puget Sound to pollutants that run off into the water and dammed waterways,

Rich salmon takes to rubs like a fish to water.

all have contributed to salmon's decline, along with overfishing. While a lot of attention has been paid recently to rehabilitating the salmon stocks in California, Oregon, and Washington, the salmon least affected by environmental factors have remained wild Alaskan salmon, the salmon we sell at Pike Place Fish and a Best Choice according to Seafood Watch.

Part of what make salmon amazing fish is that they spend time both out in the ocean (the reason for their tasty fat content) and also in freshwater rivers, where they migrate to reproduce at the end of their life cycle. Young salmon hatch in freshwater streams, then travel out to sea, where they sow their wild oats, living it up and growing to maturity. They then begin a pretty miraculous journey home, to the exact stream where they began life, using a natural GPS as accurate as any technological system developed by man. Here they become extreme athletes, forgoing food and depending on the stored oils in their flesh to survive, leaping up waterfalls and dams, hurling their bodies into the air past bear paws and swimming past hungry sea lions, all just to get home and have their own form of salmon "sex." One bummer: once the female lays her eggs, a process called spawning, she dies. After all that effort!

Though they may all look just like salmon to you, there are actually five distinct species of Pacific salmon. The runs begin in spring, with the larger and more choice king salmon appearing in May and June, which is when Seattle (and the rest of the country) goes Copper River crazy, buying up those and other "named river" fish from the icy waters of Alaska. The runs go through the summer and into early fall.

KNOW YOUR SALMON

Chinook or king salmon are the largest of the Pacific salmon. They average ten to fifteen pounds, though they can weigh more than one hundred. (We'd hate to have to throw *that* fish.) These beauties are rich in oils and omega-3s, and you can taste them.

Sockeye salmon are on the smaller end of the salmon spectrum, usually between five and eight pounds. They are less oily than chinooks, but have firmer flesh.

Coho salmon are also called silvers, and these are the salmon most frequently caught in the waters around Seattle by sports fishermen. They're a bit larger than sockeyes, and their flesh is a lighter color.

If you look closely at a package of smoked salmon, you'll probably see the term "**chum**." Chum salmon, also called keta or dog salmon, are on the larger side, averaging between ten and fifteen pounds. Their flesh is much lighter in color and less rich than kings', with a much lower oil content.

You may not have seen a **pink or humpback** salmon for sale in your market other than in a can, because that's where most of them go. Itty-bitty pinks average three to five pounds. They earned the nickname "humpback" because the males get a Quasimodo-style lump on their backs when they're spawning. Way to attract the ladies, pinky!

You'll find a host of delicious things to do with salmon in this book, from stuffing it with garlicky crab and baking it to serving it raw to basting it with an Asian-style marinade of coconut vinegar and maple syrup. Below are some of the best things we think you can do with your salmon without doing much to it at all. Soak a cedar plank and smoke it the way native tribes did for thousands of years. Forget the fillet and broil or grill a salmon steak, allowing the bones to keep the flesh moist. Or, prepare a full side of salmon the easiest way there is that guarantees a moist result: grill-poaching it in wine and lemon juice just until done. Try one, try them all, but above all, remember: these recipes work best with wild Alaskan salmon.

THE IVORY KING

White king salmon are rare, with only a few fish out of every hundred having the pale flesh that some call ivory king. Because they share the same environment and food and nearly the same flavor as their ordinary brethren, what makes their flesh white instead of that deep rosy pink that is the salmon's trademark? Scientists speculate that these fish can't metabolize the carotenoid found in the marine life that salmon eat, a substance called astaxanthin. It is this natural pigment that gives salmon its distinctive color, a color that has to be artificially induced in farmed salmon. Many claim white salmon have a more refined taste. We think all salmon are delicious, but we do agree that white salmon make for a pretty striking dish. The only trouble is, if you are buying whole fish, there is no way to know what color the flesh will be until you cut open the fish. Think of it as a delightful surprise.

SEATTLE-STYLE CEDAR-PLANKED SALMON

Now popular all over the country, cedar-planked salmon began with the local Northwest tribes who used cedar to help preserve their catch and lend it a delicious smoky taste. While you can buy planks made expressly for this purpose through Pike Place Fish's Web site and through kitchen supply stores, you can use any cedar that is untreated and not too thick.

SERVES 2

1½ cups dry white wine

3 cups water

One 1-pound wild Alaskan salmon fillet

Sea salt

Freshly cracked black pepper

Extra-virgin olive oil

Combine the white wine and water in a 13 x 9-inch baking dish. Place a 12 x 12-inch cedar plank in the pan and weigh it down with a heavy can or brick. Soak the plank for at least 1 hour.

Heat a grill to medium (too high and the wood will burn).

Season the salmon liberally with salt and pepper. Place on the cedar plank, skin side down, and drizzle with olive oil.

Place the plank on the grill rack and cook for about 10 minutes per inch of fish. The plank should smoke or steam, but you do not want huge flames. If you start to get large flames, spray with a water bottle or move the plank to a cooler part of the grill. Allow the salmon to cook through. To test for doneness, do not pierce the fish because it lets out all the juices. Instead, use a meat thermometer and cook until the inside temperature reaches 145°F.

SAM'S SIMPLE SALMON STEAKS

Though you might think of salmon fillet as king, fishmongers are just as fond of salmon steaks, knowing these cross sections of fish stay rich and juicy while cooking and really are nothing more than fillets with a little more "clothing" on. After cooking a steak, just slide out the bone and there you go: two perfect fillets! Sam likes to run his steaks under the broiler with nothing more than some great salt. If you have fancy sea salt or another kind you like, here's a great place to use it.

SERVES 4

2 salmon steaks, at least 1 inch thick
Sea salt or other good-quality salt

Preheat the broiler. Line a rimmed baking sheet with aluminum foil.

Rub each steak generously on all surfaces with salt and place on the foil-lined sheet pan.

Place 5 to 8 inches from the broiler and broil for 5 minutes. Remove the baking sheet, turn over the salmon, and return it to the broiler. Broil for 5 more minutes. Remove from the heat and allow to sit for 3 to 4 minutes. Remove the bones (and skin, if desired), divide the salmon among four plates, and serve.

GRILL-POACHED SIDE OF SALMON

This is a surprisingly uncomplicated way to cook your salmon perfectly, every time, with no mess to clean up and fish that comes cleanly off the skin. Contributor Leslie says her father, an avid salmon fisherman, cooked huge sides of freshly caught Alaskan salmon this way throughtout her childhood. Dicky cooks his in a similar way, but with a hit of garlic and sliced onions, and lemon providing all the moisture. The method below essentially poaches the salmon gently in aluminum foil on the grill. Either way, when you're done, simply ball up the foil and throw it away, skin still attached.

SERVES 6 TO 8

1 side wild Alaskan salmon fillet or large salmon fillet, skin on
Kosher salt and freshly ground black pepper
6 lemons
2 tablespoons (¼ stick) unsalted butter or extra-virgin olive oil
4 large fresh dill sprigs
Dry white wine

Preheat a grill to medium.

Using tweezers or needle-nose pliers, remove the pin bones from the salmon.

Lay out a large rectangle of aluminum foil, at least 2 inches larger than the salmon side or fillet in each direction. Sprinkle the foil with salt and pepper, then lay the salmon, skin side down, on the foil. Crimp up the edges of the foil to form a foil boat. Sprinkle the salmon with salt and pepper.

Juice 4 of the lemons. Thinly slice the remaining 2 lemons. Dot the top of the salmon with the butter or drizzle with olive oil. Lay the lemon slices, slightly overlapping, over the top of the salmon. Lay dill sprigs over the lemon slices to evenly cover the fish.

Place the foil boat directly on the grill rack. Pour the lemon juice into the foil boat and top off with the white wine. You want the liquid to come halfway up the salmon fillet, but not cover it. Cover the grill.

Cook until the salmon is just opaque in the center of the fillet, about 20 minutes. If the liquid begins to evaporate too much during cooking, add more white wine. You may use a paring knife to cut into the flesh to check for doneness.

Use a rimless baking sheet or two large spatulas to remove the foil boat from the grill. To make removal easier, lower one corner of the boat and allow any extra lemon and wine to run off before moving the fish from the grill.

Remove the lemons and dill. Use a spatula to serve portions of salmon directly from the foil boat onto individual plates; the flesh should slide easily from the skin (which will remain stuck to the foil). Serve with tartar sauce (see page 96), if you like.

SOUPS, SALADS, SANDWICHES

t's the comfort section of every menu, right? Soups, salads, and
sandwiches—a little bit of something for everyone. And indeed, we find
that the same is true here. We munch happily on updated classics like
crab cake BLTs, our own salmon patties tucked into brioche buns, and fish
burgers dredged in panko. These are more than enough on their own, which
is good because many of the soups in this section aren't the "cup on the side"
type. These are big and bold, from Caribbean seafood stew to Dad's chowder,
which is comfort in a bowl.

This is not to say you won't find lighter fare in this section. The smoked
trout salad is fresh and pretty enough to be a restaurant dish, while you could
serve your book club or your mother-in-law the shrimp salad–stuffed endive
leaves and rise to the top of everyone's list, guaranteed.

TAICHI'S TUNA SALAD

his incredible salad is like no tuna salad you've ever tasted—spicy, salty, and bright all at once, with flavors that enhance the albacore instead of weighing it down with mayo and celery. This is a staple salad at Seattle's Kappo Sushi Tamura.

SERVES 4

1 bunch mustard greens, rinsed and tough stems removed

¾ cup almonds, roasted

¾ cup sesame seeds, toasted

½ cup water

½ cup soy sauce, or more if needed

½ cup sugar

1 teaspoon wasabi paste

10 ounces skinless albacore tuna, cut into 1-inch cubes

Bring a large pan of salted water to a boil over high heat. Place a large bowl of ice water alongside the stove. When the water boils, add the mustard greens and cook just until evenly wilted and tender but still bright green, less than 1 minute. Drain the greens and add them immediately to the ice water to "shock" them (cool them down quickly). When they are cool, drain them well and pat dry on paper towels, squeezing them gently in the towels to remove excess water. Cover and refrigerate until needed.

Combine the almonds and sesame seeds in a food processor and pulse until finely ground (take care that they don't become butter). Add the ½ cup water, the soy sauce, sugar, and wasabi and process to form a smooth sauce.

Place the tuna cubes in a medium bowl and add about half of the nut sauce, tossing gently to evenly coat the tuna. If the sauce is too thick, add a teaspoon or two of soy sauce so that it more easily coats the fish.

Coarsely chop the blanched mustard greens, put them in another bowl, and toss with the remaining half of the nut sauce. Divide the mustard greens among serving plates and top with the tuna.

RECTOR'S CRAB CAKE BLT

We take it as a given that everyone knows the BLT is a great sandwich. How could you improve on such a classic? We're glad you asked. Ryan Rector says it's by adding a crab cake—that's how—made of sweet Dungeness crabmeat and our own special seasoning, right there in the middle of that bacon-and-tomato goodness. Adding a slice of cheese doesn't hurt either, the melting provolone taking it over the top.

SERVES 4

1 pound Dungeness crabmeat, picked over

3 tablespoons Northwest Seafood Seasoning (page 242)

2 large egg whites

4 green onions, chopped finely

1 red bell pepper, stemmed, seeded, and finely diced

3 tablespoons sour cream

1 cup panko (Japanese-style bread crumbs)

4 bacon strips

4 slices provolone cheese

4 soft rolls or croissants

Tartar sauce (see page 96) or mayonnaise

Sliced ripe tomato and lettuce

Combine the crabmeat, seafood seasoning, egg whites, green onions, bell pepper, and sour cream in a large bowl. Form the mixture into 4 cakes of equal size. Place the panko in a shallow bowl and dredge each patty. Place the patties on a plate and put in the freezer for 15 minutes to firm up, or chill in the fridge for up to 1 hour.

Cook the bacon in a large sauté pan over medium heat until crisp. Remove the bacon from the pan to paper towels to drain, reserving the bacon fat.

Remove the crab cakes from the freezer. In the same pan over medium heat, sauté the crab cakes in the bacon fat until golden brown on both sides and heated through, 4 to 5 minutes per side. Top each crab cake with a slice of provolone. Divide the crab cakes among the rolls and top with a slice of bacon. Garnish each sandwich with tartar sauce, tomatoes, and lettuce, as desired, and serve immediately.

HOW TO THROW A HALIBUT

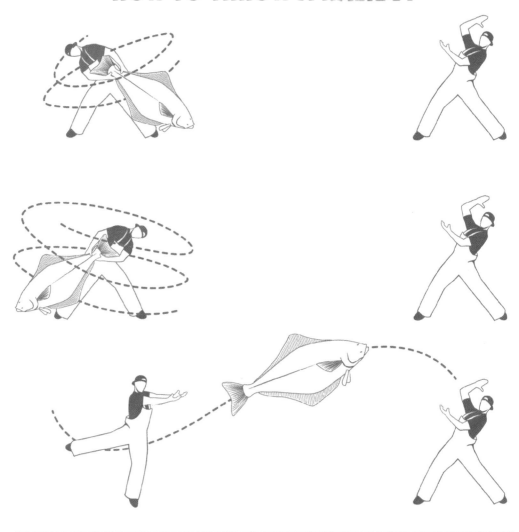

The Oh My God It's a Whole Freaking Halibut toss requires excellent core strength for catching as well as a really good wind-up to fling a twenty-pound fish skyward. Adjust the wind-up to move in either a counterclockwise or clockwise rotation depending on your dominant hand. This one's great for parties when you want to pull out all the stops.

HAPPY HALIBUT CHOWDER

Okay, maybe we're happier than the halibut is about this chowder. This is a classic soup that your family will totally dig. It's not fancy, it's just good. Gorgeous Alaskan halibut and tender potatoes in a creamy base will warm you up on those cold winter nights. Or, if you're in Seattle, really anytime but August.

SERVES 6

2 pounds halibut fillet, skin and bones removed

Kosher salt and freshly ground black pepper

6 tablespoons (¾ stick) unsalted butter

½ cup finely chopped onion

½ cup finely chopped green bell pepper

½ cup finely chopped celery

3 cups chicken broth

2 medium Yukon gold potatoes, scrubbed and cut into ½-inch cubes

2 cups half-and-half or whole milk

3 tablespoons all-purpose flour

2 tablespoons minced fresh parsley

Cut the halibut into ½-inch cubes. Sprinkle with salt and pepper and set aside.

Heat 3 tablespoons of the butter in a Dutch oven or stockpot over medium heat. Add the onion, bell pepper, and celery and sauté until soft. Add the chicken broth, bring to a simmer, and add the potatoes. Cook until the potatoes are just tender, about 10 minutes. Pour in the half-and-half and bring to a simmer. Add the halibut and check for seasoning, adding salt and pepper to taste.

While the halibut is cooking, melt the remaining 3 tablespoons of butter in a small saucepan over medium heat. Whisking constantly, add the flour, and cook for 2 to 3 minutes, taking care not to brown the flour. Transfer 1 cup of broth to the saucepan, whisking constantly, then stir the contents of the saucepan back into the chowder. Cook until slightly thickened, about 5 minutes. Serve in warmed bowls, sprinkled with parsley.

CARIBBEAN SEAFOOD STEW

This stew is so tasty and rich with coconut milk and the best seafood that you might forget that it can be ready in about twenty minutes. Reduce the jalapeño or leave it out and even young kids will happily eat it, and ask for seconds. You can add another can of tomatoes, along with a little more seasoning, if you have an unexpected guest stop in or want to stretch your dinner dollar that much further. Serve with hot cooked rice.

SERVES 4 TO 6

2 tablespoons extra-virgin olive oil

1 tablespoon fresh lime juice

3 teaspoons kosher salt

½ teaspoon freshly ground black pepper

1 pound halibut or red snapper fillets, cut into 1-inch cubes

1 medium onion, finely chopped

1 green bell pepper, stemmed, seeded, and finely chopped

6 garlic cloves, minced

1 jalapeño chile, seeded and finely chopped (or 2 if you like it hotter)

One 14.5-ounce can diced tomatoes with juice

One 14-ounce can unsweetened coconut milk

½ pound medium shrimp, peeled and deveined

½ cup chopped fresh cilantro, plus more for garnish

Bottled hot pepper sauce (optional)

Stir together 1 tablespoon of the olive oil, the lime juice, 2 teaspoons of the salt, and the pepper in a medium glass bowl. Add the fish cubes and toss to coat. Set aside.

Heat the remaining 1 tablespoon of oil in a 3-quart saucepan over medium-high heat. Add the onion, bell pepper, garlic, and jalapeño. Season with the remaining 1 teaspoon of salt. Cook and stir for 4 to 5 minutes, or until the onion is tender but not brown. Add the tomatoes and juice and the

coconut milk. Bring to a boil over high heat, then reduce the heat. Simmer, uncovered, for 10 minutes, stirring occasionally.

Stir in the shrimp, marinated fish, and cilantro. Return to a simmer and cook, uncovered, for 5 minutes, or just until the fish flakes easily with a fork and the shrimp turn opaque. Don't overcook. Taste for salt and adjust the seasoning as desired.

Ladle the stew into shallow bowls. Sprinkle with cilantro and pass hot pepper sauce, if desired.

Jake and Dan Bugge, owner of Matt's in the Market.

MATT'S GUMBO

Though we're a good distance from Cajun country, our neighbors at Matt's in the Market make a particularly fine gumbo, chock-full of catfish, sweet bay shrimp, sausage, and spices. Now, don't even think you're going to start this dish some random weeknight when you've just gotten home and you're hungry. It takes some shopping, some prep work, and then some time at the stove. But we know that any gumbo that's a pinch to put together is a gumbo not worth eating. Get your whole family or friends together and have them help out, then stick around for the result.

A couple of things to know about gumbo: it's thickened two ways—one, a flour-oil mixture called a roux and the other, a filé powder, or gumbo filé, made from sassafras leaves. Make sure you cook the roux until it's quite dark, as that adds flavor and depth. Gumbo filé can be found online. The other surprise ingredient here is dried shrimp. The shrimp can be found in Asian and Mexican markets or online.

SERVES 6

2 cups all-purpose flour

1¼ cups canola oil

2 red onions, cut into medium dice

2 large celery stalks, cut into medium dice

2 poblano chiles, cut into medium dice

1 Fresno chile, cut into small dice

2 red bell peppers, cut into medium dice

4 garlic cloves, minced

1 teaspoon dried thyme

1 teaspoon dried oregano

1 teaspoon cayenne pepper

1 tablespoon dried shrimp

3 tablespoons gumbo filé

6 quarts hot chicken broth

1 pound cooked spicy Italian or andouille sausage, sliced

1 pound catfish, cut into 1-inch dice

¼ pound roasted chicken, chopped

3 to 4 fresh thyme sprigs, leaves stripped and minced

3 to 4 fresh oregano sprigs, leaves stripped and minced

Louisiana hot sauce, such as Trappey's

Fresh lemon juice

Kosher salt and freshly ground black pepper

1 cup cooked bay shrimp

½ cup chopped green onions

Preheat the oven to 450°F.

Begin by making the roux. Place the flour in a small bowl. Add 1 cup of the canola oil in small increments, stirring the mixture with a fork. In the end you will need 1½ cups of roux that is the consistency of wet sand. Adjust the ratio, adding more oil if necessary, to achieve the correct consistency.

Place the roux in an ovenproof sauté pan or pot. Roast in the oven, stirring every 5 minutes, or until the roux is a deep brown. Set aside the roux and turn off the oven.

Add 2 tablespoons of the remaining canola oil to a large stockpot. Place over medium-high heat. Add the red onions and celery and cook for 2 to 3 minutes, or until soft. Add the poblano chiles, Fresno chile, and bell peppers and cook for 2 to 3 minutes more. Stir in the garlic, dried thyme, dried oregano, and cayenne. Add the dried shrimp and cook for 2 minutes. Add the filé and mix well so that there are no clumps. Stir in 1 cup of the reserved roux. Slowly whisk in the hot chicken broth and bring to a simmer. Add the sausage, catfish, and chicken, as well as the fresh thyme and oregano.

Stir in up to ½ cup of the remaining roux for thickening. Simmer for 20 minutes. Just before serving, add hot sauce, lemon juice, salt, and black pepper to taste. Ladle into shallow bowls and garnish each bowl with bay shrimp and green onions.

DILLED SMOKED TROUT SALAD WITH PEAS AND GRAPES

This is the salad for spring, when you want to eat something fresh and light. Whether you smoke your own or buy it already prepared, smoked trout generally has a pretty delicate flavor and so it's nice not to overwhelm it with heavy ingredients. Add some bread and call this lunch.

Frisée is a curly, frizzy pale green that has a cool texture and a mildly bitter edge to it. If you can't find it or don't care for the bitterness, you can substitute another type of lettuce or green. The salad is best if there is a combination of flavors and textures in the greens.

SERVES 4

1 cup red seedless grapes
1 cup cherry tomatoes

6 cups torn red leaf lettuce

2 cups torn frisée

1 cup shelled English peas

¼ cup extra-virgin olive oil

Kosher salt

2 teaspoons sherry vinegar

½ lemon

Freshly ground black pepper

8 ounces smoked trout, flaked

2 teaspoons minced fresh dill

Cut the grapes in half lengthwise. Cut the cherry tomatoes in half or in quarters, if large. You want the fruits and vegetables to be roughly the same size.

Place the red leaf lettuce and frisée in a large bowl. Add the peas, grapes, and tomatoes. Drizzle with the olive oil and add a pinch of salt. Toss to coat the ingredients evenly. Sprinkle with the vinegar and squeeze the lemon over. Toss to coat. Adjust the salt as needed and add pepper to taste.

Divide the salad among four plates or shallow bowls. Sprinkle each with some of the smoked trout and dill. Serve immediately.

PIPIN' HOT CAJUN CATFISH SANDWICHES

Chris likes it hot, especially when you're talking about these catfish sandwiches. The panko-cornmeal coating keeps the fish good and crispy, making for the best catfish sandwich this side of Louisiana. Adjust the seasonings to taste or substitute a pinch or two of our Cajun and Blackening Seasoning instead of the cayenne and chili powder. It's nice if the bread you use is soft, but please don't break out the Wonder bread for this. In New Orleans, they'd run you out of town on a rail for a lot less.

SERVES 4

1 cup cornmeal

1 cup panko

Pinch cayenne pepper

Pinch chili powder

2 teaspoons dried oregano

Kosher salt and freshly ground black pepper

1 cup buttermilk

4 catfish fillets (about 1⅓ pounds)

2 tablespoons of canola oil

8 slices soft white bread or 4 buns, cut in half

½ cup mayonnaise (make it spicy by adding more cayenne and chili powder, if you like)

Lettuce and tomato

Preheat the oven to 450°F.

Combine the cornmeal, panko, cayenne, chili powder, oregano, salt, and pepper in a shallow bowl. Place the buttermilk in a shallow bowl. Dip the catfish into the buttermilk, then into the cornmeal mixture.

Heat a large ovenproof sauté pan over medium-high heat until hot but not smoking. Pour the canola oil into the bottom of the pan and swirl to coat.

Add the catfish and sear each side for 2 minutes, or until golden brown. Place the sauté pan in the oven and bake for 5 minutes or until cooked through.

Place the fillets on 4 pieces of the bread or on one half of each bun. Spread with mayonnaise and layer with lettuce and tomato. Add salt and black pepper to taste, top with bread, and enjoy.

Miso soup with clams provided by Mashiko restaurant.

MISO SOUP WITH CLAMS

This soup is adapted from one served by the Seattle Japanese restaurant Mashiko, which served as our mentor during our shift to totally sustainable seafood. Hot and tempting, the soup is both delicate and totally full of amazing, rich flavors. The combination of miso and butter, especially, adds depth to the briny flavor of the clams. Kombu is a type of dried kelp and is available at Asian markets or online. Red miso paste has a stronger flavor than white. Though using both misos is nice, you can use just white if that's all you can find.

SERVES 8 AS A FIRST COURSE

2 quarts water

1 sheet kombu, 5 to 6 inches long

2 to 3 dried shiitake mushrooms

4 fresh shiitake mushrooms

¾ cup white miso paste

¼ cup red miso paste

1 to 1½ pounds Manila clams (about 4 clams per person), washed well

2 tablespoons mirin (sweet rice wine) or more to taste

3 tablespoons unsalted butter

Combine the water, kombu, and dried shiitakes in a large stockpot over high heat. Bring to a boil, then lower the heat to a simmer and cook for 10 to 15 minutes. Wipe the fresh shiitakes clean and cut off the tough ends of the stems. Thinly slice the mushrooms.

Remove the kombu and shiitakes from the pot and discard. Whisk the white and red miso pastes into the broth in the pot until completely dissolved. Lower the heat to maintain the lowest possible simmer; do not allow the miso to boil. Add the clams and fresh shiitakes to the miso broth and cook for 2 to 3 minutes, or until the clams just open. Stir in the mirin. Taste and add more mirin to balance the flavors, if needed.

Divide the broth, mushrooms, and clams among eight bowls. Top each bowl with about 1 teaspoon of butter. Serve immediately.

Anders and Jaison take a break near a fave Market neighbor, restaurant Place Pigalle.

BOUILLABAISSE DE PLACE PIGALLE

A true Mediterranean masterpiece, bouillabaisse is one of life's great pleasures—the freshest fish and seafood in a delicate broth scented with white wine. This special recipe comes from our French neighbors at the Market, the restaurant Place Pigalle. It serves two generously, and may be doubled. Use whatever fresh fish and seafood look best or are recommended by your fishmonger.

SERVES 2

1 tablespoon extra-virgin olive oil

1 medium onion, cut into julienne

6 large garlic cloves, thinly sliced

2 cups dry white wine

One 16-ounce can crushed tomatoes

2 quarts fish fumet, chicken broth, bottled clam nectar, or a combination

Pinch Spanish saffron threads

Kosher salt and freshly ground black pepper

¼ pound mussels, debearded and rinsed

¼ pound clams, washed well

¼ pound whitefish, diced

3 fingerling potatoes, boiled or steamed, thickly sliced

¼ pound prawns, peeled and deveined

2 or 3 squid bodies, sliced, or cracked crab claws (optional)

1 tablespoon unsalted butter

Fresh lemon juice

2 teaspoons mixed chopped fresh herbs, such as parsley, chives, and thyme

Begin by making a broth. Heat the olive oil in a large saucepan or stockpot over medium heat. Add the onion and garlic and cook until tender and translucent. Deglaze the pan with the white wine, scraping up bits from the bottom of the pan. Add the tomatoes, fish fumet, broth, or nectar and saffron. Bring to a boil, over high heat, then reduce the heat to a simmer, and cook for 30 minutes. Add salt and pepper to taste.

When ready to serve, place 3 cups of saffron broth in a large sauté pan, thinning the broth with white wine if it seems too thick. Add the mussels, clams, whitefish, potatoes, and prawns. Bring to a simmer. As they finish cooking, remove the fish and shellfish to two heated bowls, dividing some of each between each bowl. The whitefish should just turn opaque and the mussels and clams should open. Add the squid and crab (if using) to the broth remaining in the pan and cook just until the squid is opaque and the crab is heated through. Remove and divide between the bowls. Add the butter and lemon juice to taste to the broth remaining in the pan. Taste for seasoning, then pour the broth over the seafood in the bowls. Garnish each bowl with fresh herbs and serve immediately.

DAD'S SEAFOOD CHOWDER

This happens to be an adaptation of Anders' dad's recipe, though it seems right to us that Anders' dad, your dad, our dads would all be the kind of men to make a big pot of soothing chowder like this one. Use whatever seafood looks best in the market, combining different textures and flavors to add interest. This makes enough chowder for a hungry army, but we think no one would mind batting cleanup the next day with a steaming bowlful for lunch.

SERVES 6 TO 8

6 cups peeled, diced waxy potatoes, such as red potatoes or Yukon golds

8 tablespoons (1 stick) unsalted butter

6 bacon strips, chopped

4 cups chopped sweet onions, such as Walla Walla

3 shallots, chopped

2 cups thinly sliced celery

2 garlic cloves, minced

6 green onions, finely chopped

2 teaspoons dried dill

1 teaspoon freshly ground black pepper, or more to taste

Kosher salt

6 cups mixed seafood, such as halibut chunks, black cod or lingcod, salmon, shrimp, scallops, clams, or mussels

2 cups chicken broth

2 quarts half-and-half

¼ cup chopped fresh parsley

Bring a large pot of salted water to a boil over high heat. Add the potatoes and cook until just tender, about 10 minutes. Drain, rinse with cold water, and set aside.

In a large stockpot or Dutch oven, melt the butter over medium-high heat. Add the bacon and sautè until brown. Add the sweet onions, shallots, celery, garlic, green onions, dill, pepper, and salt to taste. Cook, stirring frequently, until the vegetables are soft, 6 to 8 minutes. Add the seafood and chicken broth to the pot. Cover and simmer over low heat for 10 minutes, or until the shellfish have opened and the fish are cooked through.

Pour in the half-and-half and add the potatoes. Simmer for 10 to 15 minutes. Taste for salt and pepper and adjust the seasonings. Right before serving, stir in the parsley.

MATT'S FISH BURGERS

Instead of making plain old burgers next time you get the gang together, how about delicious fish burgers as a change of pace? Snapper fillets get pureed with aromatics and herbs, coated in panko, then take a quick turn in a hot oven. This recipe comes from our neighbor Matt's in the Market and has been making lunch goers happy for years.

SERVES 6

2½ pounds snapper or rockfish fillets, pin bones removed with
    tweezers or needle-nose pliers

3 tablespoons extra-virgin olive oil

½ cup diced sweet onion, such as Walla Walla

½ cup diced celery

4 slices white sandwich bread

1 tablespoon chopped fresh parsley

1 tablespoon chopped fresh chives

1 tablespoon fresh lemon juice

2 large eggs

¼ cup mayonnaise

2 cups panko

6 buns, preferably brioche

Red onion rings

Tartar sauce (see page 96)

Lettuce and tomato slices

Preheat the oven to 350°F.

Place the snapper in a food processor and blend into a paste. Transfer to a bowl and set aside.

Heat 1 tablespoon of the olive oil in a medium sauté pan over medium-high heat. Add the onion and celery and sauté until translucent, but not yet browned. Tear the sandwich bread into pieces and place in the food processor. Pulse into crumbs. Add the onion mixture, parsley, chives, lemon juice, eggs, and mayonnaise. Pulse to combine. Add the snapper and puree into a thick paste.

Form the mixture into 6 patties. Place the panko on a plate and dip each patty into the panko to coat. In a large ovenproof skillet, heat the remaining 2 tablespoons olive oil. Add the patties and sear on each side for 1½ minutes, or until golden brown. Place the skillet in the oven and bake for about 5 minutes, or until the patties are cooked through. Serve on brioche buns with red onion, tartar sauce, lettuce, and tomatoes, as desired.

SHRIMP SALAD WITH ENDIVE

Sweet little bay shrimp are a delicious and economical favorite of ours, especially in salads like this one brightened with a touch of licorice-y fennel. This is elegant finger food when served in individual endive leaves—like tea party elegant. If you prefer, spoon the salad into half of a ripe, creamy avocado for a delicious and rich lunch. To keep the fennel from discoloring after slicing, toss with a bit of lemon juice.

SERVES 12 TO 16

1 teaspoon kosher salt

Juice of ½ lemon

1 tablespoon extra-virgin olive oil

¼ cup diced fennel bulb, plus some of the fronds for garnish

½ pound cooked bay shrimp

3 heads Belgian endive

½ ripe avocado, peeled, pitted, and diced

Dissolve the salt in the lemon juice in a medium bowl. Whisk in the olive oil. Add the fennel and shrimp and toss to coat. Take 1 of the heads of endive and slice crosswise into thin ribbons. Add the sliced endive and avocado to the bowl and gently combine.

Trim the base of each of the 2 remaining heads of endive. Separate the leaves and arrange on a platter. Divide the shrimp salad among the leaves. Chop a couple of tablespoons of fennel fronds and sprinkle evenly over the top.

PIKE PLACE FISH SALMON PATTIES

These are the very same patties that seem to fly out of the case at Pike Place Fish. They are great served on their own or with your favorite sauce, such as tartar or dill sauce. We think the best way to serve them is on a brioche bun, with a little arugula, tomato, and a slice of Walla Walla sweet onion on top. This might be the best salmon burger ever.

SERVES 4

1 pound boneless, skinless wild salmon, finely chopped

4 teaspoons avocado or extra-virgin olive oil

1 tablespoon Our Own Rub (page 248)

1 teaspoon Northwest Seafood Seasoning (page 242)

1 cup panko

Place the chopped salmon in a large bowl and add 2 teaspoons of the avocado oil, the rub, and the seafood seasoning. Mix thoroughly with your hands. Add the panko and mix to combine.

Form the mixture evenly into 4 patties, packing them firmly around the edges so they don't fall apart (we use a burger press at the shop). Each patty should be between ½ and ¾ inch thick.

Preheat a skillet (cast iron works well) over medium heat for 5 to 10 minutes. Add the remaining 2 teaspoons of avocado oil and swirl to coat the bottom of the pan. When the oil is nearly smoking, add the patties and cook for 3 minutes. Turn carefully with a spatula and cook for another 2 to 3 minutes. The patties may also be grilled over medium-high heat for the same amount of time.

TUESDAY-NIGHT TUNA

n our parents' day, Tuesday-Night Tuna would have meant a chapter full of casseroles made with canned fish. For those of you who still have a thing for tuna casserole (with crunchy noodles on top), we mean no disrespect, but you won't find a lot of those recipes here.

Why not? Because, simply put, there is no need to use canned fish and canned soup to make a quick dinner any Tuesday night, whether it's for you and your cat or for your hungry family of six. Instead, you could whip up Filipino-style squid, quick simmered in soy sauce and vinegar; bake salmon in a coconut-maple glaze; sauté some halibut cheeks with an eggplant relish; make fish tacos with fresh rockfish, topped with a creamy mango drizzle; or cook up our version of shrimp and grits. These are the recipes we make at home and dishes we serve to our families, with a smattering of excellent submissions from customers—from home cooks to restaurants—thrown in to make things even more exciting.

We talk to lots of people who don't have a seafood or fish dish in their regular weekly rotation. Often, it's because they want ideas about where to start. Here we provide you with an incredible array of ideas, from five-minute fast to fancier recipes that could just as easily serve company as family. The truth is, for those of you looking for the dinner option for a busy weekday, there is often no food quicker to get on the table than fish or seafood, and it's great for you on top of it all. We hope you find the recipes in Tuesday-Night Tuna useful, delicious, and inspiring.

ADOBONG PUSIT

This delicious squid is a family recipe that comes from Jaison's in-laws. It has the hallmarks of Filipino food—soy, garlic, and vinegar. When making the dish, remember the rule about how to keep squid tender: either cook it quickly or cook it for a long time over low heat. Anything in the middle and you're talking rubber. Add some hot rice and this is home-cooked fast food, Filipino style.

SERVES 4

3 to 4 garlic cloves, minced

⅓ cup white vinegar

⅓ cup soy sauce

¼ cup water

1 teaspoon sugar

1 small bay leaf

1½ teaspoons kosher salt

¼ teaspoon freshly ground black pepper

1 pound squid bodies and tentacles, cleaned

3 tablespoons vegetable oil

2 Roma tomatoes, chopped

1 small onion, thinly sliced

Combine half of the garlic, the vinegar, soy sauce, water, sugar, bay leaf, salt, and pepper in a medium bowl. Add the squid and marinate for 1 hour. Drain the squid, reserving the marinade.

Heat the vegetable oil in a large skillet over medium heat. Add the remaining half of the garlic and sauté until fragrant, about 1 minute. Stir in the tomatoes and onion. Stir-fry 2 to 3 minutes, until soft and wilted. Add the drained squid and cook, stirring, for 1 to 2 minutes. Add the reserved marinade. Increase the heat and bring the liquid to a boil, then immediately lower the heat to a simmer. Taste for seasonings. Alternatively, for a drier dish you may also allow the liquid to come to a simmer and cook gently for 30 to 45 minutes. Remove from the heat and transfer to a serving dish.

SAUTÉED HALIBUT CHEEKS WITH CAPONATA AND POACHED EGGS

As far as we're concerned, fresh halibut cheeks are one of the most killer fish you can buy. Fish this good deserves nothing but the best accompaniments, and longtime Pike Place Fish customer The Van Camp House restaurant in Port Sanilac, Michigan, got it right with this one. Sautéed halibut cheeks are nestled on a pool of caponata—a Sicilian sweet-sour relish—then topped with a poached egg. Break the yolk and let it run over the fish and mix with the silky vegetables. Heaven.

SERVES 4

1 red bell pepper

1 medium globe eggplant, peeled

½ cup extra-virgin olive oil, plus 2 tablespoons for frying

1 medium sweet onion, such as Walla Walla or Vidalia, cut into small dice

2 celery stalks, cut into small dice

3 garlic cloves, minced

½ cup small capers, rinsed and drained

Pinch crushed red pepper flakes

Kosher salt and freshly ground black pepper

2 tablespoons sherry vinegar

8 halibut cheeks, preferably fresh

½ cup all-purpose flour

4 large eggs

Roast the bell pepper under a broiler or over an open gas flame until blackened all over. Wrap tightly in aluminum foil or place in a paper bag and allow to sit for 10 minutes. Rub off the blackened skin and discard the stem and seeds. Dice the flesh and set aside.

Cut the eggplant into ¼-inch dice. Warm a stainless-steel pan over medium heat. Add the 2 tablespoons of olive oil, then the onion, celery, and eggplant.

When the vegetables begin to brown lightly, add the garlic, roasted red pepper, capers, and red pepper flakes. Cook, stirring, over low to medium-low heat until soft. Season with salt and pepper to taste. Stir in the vinegar. Remove the caponata to a small container and cover with the ½ cup of olive oil. (Can be stored in the refrigerator in a glass jar with a tight-fitting lid. Just remember to add extra olive oil to the jar to ensure the mixture is covered.)

Pat the halibut cheeks dry and season with salt and pepper. Dredge the cheeks in flour, knocking off any excess. Film the bottom of a large sauté pan with olive oil and heat over medium-high heat. Add the cheeks and sauté until golden brown, 2 to 3 minutes per side. Keep warm.

Either poach or soft-fry the eggs in a bit of olive oil. Place a large spoonful of caponata on each of four plates. Top with 2 halibut cheeks, followed by an egg.

SPOT PRAWNS AND GRAVY WITH POLENTA

There are various schools of thought on the proper way to prepare polenta. We like a lot of cheese and butter in ours, and like it even better when it is made with a quick prawn stock. The "gravy" is what makes it, though, and it's super delicious and easy to make.

SERVES 4

Polenta

2 tablespoons (¼ stick) unsalted butter

Shells from 1 pound spot prawns (below)

5 cups water

1 cup instant polenta

1 cup grated Parmesan or pecorino cheese

Kosher salt and freshly ground black pepper

4 bacon strips, chopped

1 cup finely chopped green bell pepper

1 medium onion, finely chopped

3 to 4 garlic cloves, minced

1 teaspoon dried thyme

1 teaspoon fennel seed or dried tarragon

Kosher salt and freshly cracked black pepper

1 pound spot prawns, peeled and shells reserved for polenta

3 tablespoons cold unsalted butter

To make the polenta, heat 1 tablespoon of the butter in a deep saucepan over medium heat. Add the prawn shells and sauté, stirring, until the shells change color. Add the water, bring to a boil over high heat, then lower the heat to a simmer. Cook for 15 minutes. Strain the stock and measure out 4½ cups. Add water, if needed. Discard the shells.

Rinse out the saucepan and bring the stock to a boil over high heat. Slowly whisk in the polenta, adding it in a slow, steady stream. Reduce the heat to low and keep stirring, making sure the polenta isn't sticking to the bottom of the pan. When the polenta thickens, whisk in the Parmesan, then the remaining 1 tablespoon butter. Season with salt and pepper.

To make the spot prawns, fry the bacon in a medium sauté pan over medium heat until crispy. Remove the bacon with a slotted spoon to drain on paper towels, reserving the fat in the pan. Add the bell pepper, onion, and garlic and sauté over medium heat until soft. Add the thyme and fennel seed and season with salt and pepper.

Add the spot prawns to the pan. The prawns will give off liquid; stir to incorporate. Cook until the prawns are bright pink. Add the butter in 3 pieces, stirring until the sauce is glossy and the butter is incorporated. Serve over polenta, sprinkled with the reserved bacon.

ALBACORE TUNA SLIDERS

This quick, easy, and delicious recipe features a seared whole piece of tuna loin that's seared on a grill and then cut into slices and slid into brioche buns. Okay, so these are also technically sandwiches. If you're wondering why these sliders are here instead of in the previous chapter, there are two reasons. The first is that Anders thought there needed to be a tuna option in Tuesday-Night Tuna. But the other reason is less pedantic: these are easy to make on a weeknight and make a fantastic dinner for four. Anders serves these with Pike Place Fish Smoked Walla Walla Onion Tartar Sauce, but you can serve it with any tartar-style sauce.

SERVES 4

1 pound albacore tuna loin (ask for a piece off the front end, for even thickness)

2 tablespoons soy sauce

2 tablespoons extra-virgin olive oil

2 tablespoons Northwest Seafood Seasoning (page 242)

½ teaspoon crushed red pepper flakes

Slider buns, brioche, if possible

1 medium heirloom tomato or other ripe beefsteak tomato, thinly sliced

Arugula leaves, rinsed and dried

Tartar sauce, such as Pike Place Fish Smoked Walla Walla Onion Tartar Sauce

Remove the skin from the tuna and score the flesh every inch with a knife, as if you were making steaks. Repeat on all sides, but make sure not to cut all the way through.

Mix the soy sauce, olive oil, seafood seasoning, and red pepper flakes in a small bowl. Using a basting brush, brush the mixture on all sides of the tuna, making sure to get some marinade inside the scored parts of the fish, so it's well coated. Marinate at room temperature for 15 to 20 minutes.

Preheat a grill to high. Make sure the grates are clean and well oiled. Put the tuna directly on the grill and cook for about 2 to 3 minutes on each side, or 6 minutes total for rare. During the last minute of cooking, toast the buns on the grill. Slice the tuna into four sections along score lines. Serve on the buns with sliced tomato, arugula, and your favorite condiment.

ROCKFISH TACOS WITH MANGO AIOLI

Anders likes to serve this zesty rockfish dish straight on the plate, but we couldn't resist tucking the lime-accented fish into tortillas and then drizzling them with Taho's magnificent Mango Aioli, for a killer sweet-sour effect. It makes for a nice cross-fishmonger "Kumbaya" moment and for one delicious dinner.

SERVES 4 TO 6

½ cup finely chopped fresh cilantro
½ cup finely diced white onion
2 cups shredded cabbage
Kosher salt and freshly ground black pepper
2 pounds rockfish or snapper fillets, cut into 6 to 8 pieces
4 tablespoons flour
2 tablespoons extra-virgin olive oil
Zest and juice of 2 limes
1 cup dry white wine
1 package flour tortillas
Mango Aioli (page 239)

Combine the cilantro and onion in a small bowl and set aside. In another small bowl, lightly toss the cabbage with salt and set aside to soften a bit.

Sprinkle the rockfish evenly with flour, salt, and pepper. Heat the olive oil in a large sauté pan over medium-high heat until hot but not smoking. Add the fish and cook for 4 to 5 minutes, or until golden brown on the bottom. Turn the fish and add the lime zest, lime juice, and white wine, swirling the pan to mix the juices. Reduce the heat to medium and continue to cook for another 4 to 5 minutes, or until the fish is flaky. Remove the fish to a platter.

Serve the fish in the tortillas and allow guests to add the cabbage and the cilantro mixture as desired. Drizzle with the Mango Aioli to taste.

COCONUT MAPLE SALMON

The coconut flavor in this extremely easy, tasty dish comes from an unlikely source: coconut vinegar. Made from fermented coconut water—the liquid sloshing around inside fresh coconuts—coconut vinegar is mild and almost sweet. You can find it at Asian markets or online. Use it in marinades for other fish, and it's terrific with pork. Please use real maple syrup in this dish. Artificial syrup is too sweet and won't give the sauce the balance it needs.

SERVES 4

½ cup soy sauce

½ cup real maple syrup

¼ cup coconut vinegar

2 garlic cloves, thinly sliced

1 jalapeño or serrano chile, deribbed and minced (optional)

2 pounds salmon fillets, skin on

Combine the soy sauce, maple syrup, coconut vinegar, garlic, and jalapeño (if using) in a glass bowl. Add the salmon, skin side up, so that the flesh is submerged in the marinade. Cover and place in the fridge for at least 30 minutes or up to 1 hour to marinate. Remove from the fridge at least 15 minutes before baking.

Preheat the oven to 350°F.

Remove the salmon from the marinade and transfer to a glass baking dish, skin side down. Pour the marinade over the salmon. Bake for about 20 minutes, basting with the marinade halfway through the cooking time. The salmon is done when it is moist and flaky and barely opaque in the center. Do not overcook. Allow to rest for 5 minutes before serving.

AUNTY LYNN'S STURGEON WITH MANGO SALSA

Jaison can wax poetic about each and every dish created by his dear aunt, Lynn Scott, as being incredible. He remembers her as a creative soul whose generous spirit was reflected in the vibrant, flavorful dishes she loved making (and he, of course, loved eating!). We think you'll agree when you see the way she had around mild sturgeon, spicing it with a touch of chili powder and anise, then scattering a colorful mango salsa over the top. The salsa would also be good on other types of simply prepared fish, from rockfish to tuna.

SERVES 4

2 medium ripe mangoes, peeled, pitted, and diced

2 medium apples (any kind), peeled, cored, and diced

1 large sweet or red onion, diced

1 teaspoon crushed red pepper flakes

1 cup finely chopped fresh cilantro

1 celery stalk, finely chopped

Juice of 2 lemons or limes

1 teaspoon balsamic vinegar

Coarse sea salt and freshly ground black pepper

Four 1-inch-thick sturgeon steaks

2 tablespoons extra-virgin olive oil, plus more for the steaks

Chili powder

Aniseed

Combine the mangoes, apples, onion, red pepper flakes, cilantro, celery, lemon juice, balsamic vinegar, and salt and pepper to taste in a large bowl. Let the salsa sit, covered, in the fridge for 30 minutes.

Rub each sturgeon steak on both sides with a film of olive oil. Dust with chili powder, salt, and pepper. Add a pinch of aniseed to each.

Heat the olive oil in a heavy skillet over medium-high heat. When the oil is hot but not smoking, place the sturgeon steaks in the skillet and sear on each side for 4 to 5 minutes, or until cooked through. Transfer to four individual plates and add a scoop of salsa to each steak.

JUSTIN'S CRAB-STUFFED KING SALMON

Just the thing for a company dinner or a large family gathering, luscious salmon stuffed with creamy crab makes everyone's hit list. And the recipe couldn't be easier, leaving you time for talking with your guests. If you can get your hands on white salmon, the dish is especially attractive, but trust us that it tastes great either way.

SERVES 6 TO 8

One 4-pound king salmon fillet

Kosher salt and freshly ground black pepper

¾ pound fresh crabmeat, picked over

3 large garlic cloves, finely chopped

Two 8-ounce packages cream cheese, softened

6 green onions, minced

1 lemon, scrubbed and sliced thinly into rings

Preheat the oven to 400°F.

Take the salmon out of the refrigerator at least 15 minutes before stuffing to allow the fish to come to room temperature.

Using a sharp knife, make a vertical slice in the salmon fillet, taking care not to cut all the way through and creating a pocket for the stuffing. Season the fish on both sides with salt and pepper.

Combine the crabmeat, garlic, cream cheese, and green onions in a medium bowl. Season with salt and pepper.

Stuff the crab mixture into the pocket of the fish. Use toothpicks to secure the cut edge and keep the filling from spilling out. Place the salmon in a baking dish and overlap the lemon slices on top. Bake for 25 to 30 minutes, or until the stuffing is hot and the salmon just flakes to the touch.

YORI'S GRANDMA'S COD CAKES

These lovely cod cakes don't look their best when you're whipping them up in the food processor. Yori warned us about this—but don't lose heart! Once they're golden brown, they're pretty irresistible to nearly everyone, even noncoastal people who aren't as used to eating fish, and kids will enjoy them happily for dinner. Serve with your favorite sauce for dipping.

SERVES 4

1 pound true or lingcod fillets

1½ teaspoons kosher salt

½ cup whole milk

4 teaspoons all-purpose flour

2 tablespoons fresh tarragon leaves

1 tablespoon canola oil

1 tablespoon unsalted butter

MEET YOUR FISHMONGER

YORI OYLOE: YEARS AS A FISHMONGER: 13 FAVORITE SEAFOOD: FATTY KING SALMON

Place the cod and salt in the bowl of a food processor and process until smooth. Gradually add the milk to form a smooth paste. Add the flour and tarragon and pulse to combine.

Heat the canola oil and butter in a large nonstick skillet over medium heat. Swirl to combine the fats and coat the bottom of the pan.

Using two spoons or a small cookie scoop with a release, form the fish paste into 16 balls. Place the balls in the skillet and flatten each slightly with a spatula into a cake. Cook for 5 minutes, turn, then cook for 5 more minutes, or until cooked through and golden brown. Serve immediately.

MASHIKO SCALLOPS WITH DUNGENESS CRAB

Mashiko, a fully sustainable Seattle Japanese restaurant, has the magic touch with simple, elegant dishes that knock your socks off. This recipe is one of them, rich with butter and crab but somehow still light and flavorful. You will want to use larger sea scallops, like the Alaskan weathervanes we sell, not smaller bay scallops.

SERVES 2

4 tablespoons (½ stick) unsalted butter

6 large sea scallops

½ teaspoon grated fresh ginger

½ teaspoon minced garlic

1 teaspoon soy sauce

¼ lemon

⅓ pound Dungeness crabmeat, picked over

Daikon radish sprouts, for garnish

Heat the butter in a medium sauté pan, over medium-high heat. When the butter is bubbling, add the scallops and cook without moving them for 1 minute. Turn the scallops and sear the other side. Remove from the pan and place on two warmed plates.

Add the ginger, garlic, soy sauce, and a squeeze of the lemon to the same pan. Swirl the liquid in the pan over medium heat and lightly scrape up any bits stuck to the bottom of the pan. Add the crab and mix gently to combine. Turn out the crab mixture onto the scallops, dividing evenly. Garnish with daikon radish sprouts and serve immediately.

SPICY SWORDFISH STEAKS

We love the meaty texture of swordfish, great for grilling, and the way it stands up to bold flavors like capers, olives, and garlic. Adjust the hot sauce and crushed red pepper flakes to suit your own tastes. This dish is good with both briny black olives or flavorful green ones, stuffed or no. Use the recipe as a guide and come up with your own creation.

SERVES 4

3 tablespoons extra-virgin olive oil

¼ cup diced yellow onion

2 garlic cloves, minced

3 medium tomatoes, seeded and chopped

1 teaspoon bottled hot sauce

¼ cup pitted and chopped briny black olives, such as Niçoise, or green olives

2 tablespoons red wine vinegar

2 tablespoons chopped capers

2 teaspoons fresh thyme

4 pieces swordfish steak (2 pounds)

Kosher salt

¼ teaspoon crushed red pepper flakes

Heat 2 tablespoons of the olive oil in a small saucepan over medium-high heat. Add onion and garlic and cook until softened but not browned. Add the tomatoes, hot sauce, olives, vinegar, capers, and thyme. Simmer for 5 to 8 minutes to combine the flavors. Set aside.

Preheat a grill to medium-high. Rub the swordfish with the remaining 1 tablespoon olive oil and season with salt and red pepper flakes. Place on the grill and cook for 8 to 10 minutes, or until just opaque.

Serve the swordfish steaks with the room-temperature sauce spooned over them.

MASCARPONE-BAKED SALMON WITH HERBS

Even though salmon is a rich fish, it takes well to accompaniments like the satiny, sinful Italian cheese called mascarpone. If you've never had it, trust us that it's like cream and clouds had a lovechild. Pike Place Fish–fan Rachel knows this cheese quite well and uses it to full advantage in this recipe. The mixed herbs add brightness to the dish, balancing the dairy and creating a luscious sauce.

If you can't find mascarpone, you may substitute cream cheese mixed with a bit of heavy cream. This recipe makes a bit more sauce than is necessary for the salmon. You can spoon reserved sauce on top of the fish when serving, or do as we do and use it, mixed with a bit of cream cheese if you like, as a dip for vegetables or crackers.

SERVES 4

8 ounces mascarpone cheese

4 ounces plain Greek yogurt

1 tablespoon honey

¼ cup extra-virgin olive oil

Leaves from 1 bunch fresh cilantro, rinsed and dried, 2 tablespoons reserved for garnish

1 avocado, peeled, pitted, and flesh removed

Zest and juice of 2 limes

Small handful fresh parsley

1 tablespoon fresh thyme

2 tablespoons fresh basil, chopped

1 tablespoon kosher salt

2 pounds salmon fillets

1 cup chopped, toasted pistachio nuts

Preheat the oven to 350°F.

Combine the mascarpone, yogurt, honey, olive oil, cilantro, avocado, lime

zest, lime juice, parsley, thyme, basil, and salt in a food processor or blender and puree until creamy.

Spread 1½ cups of the sauce in the bottom of a casserole dish or baking dish large enough to fit the fillets. Place the salmon fillets, skin side up, on top. Marinate at room temperature for 20 minutes.

Pop the casserole as is into the oven and bake for 20 minutes, or until the salmon just flakes when pricked with a fork. Remove the skin and garnish the fish with the reserved cilantro and the toasted pistachio nuts.

BAKED PACIFIC OYSTERS WITH CHORIZO, SPINACH, AND BLACK TRUMPET MUSHROOM GRATIN

Full disclosure: this is one of the more involved dishes in this chapter, hailing from Anthony Polizzi at the market's neighboring Steelhead Diner. However, once you taste these sweet-briny oysters stuffed with a chorizo cream, all mingling with silky mushrooms and spinach and crowned with a Parmesan–bread crumb sprinkle, we defy you to argue that this restaurant dish isn't worth the trouble of re-creating at home. Save it for the weekend if you must, but trust us and make it.

Black trumpet mushrooms have an incredible smoky flavor, and they look cool, but they can be hard to find. Chanterelles would make a great substitute, or even fresh shiitakes, but avoid using button mushrooms. The texture and flavor just don't quite work.

SERVES 4 AS AN ENTRÉE OR 6 AS AN APPETIZER

12 tablespoons extra-virgin olive oil

4 cups black trumpet mushrooms, wiped clean

Kosher salt and freshly ground black pepper

¾ cup dried bread crumbs

¼ cup grated Parmesan cheese

2 tablespoons chopped fresh parsley

4 links Spanish-style chorizo, casings removed

½ cup finely diced yellow onion

¼ cup finely diced celery

¼ cup finely diced leek

1 tablespoon chopped garlic

2 tablespoons all-purpose flour

¼ cup dry sherry

2 cups heavy cream

3 cups baby spinach

½ teaspoon white pepper

1 teaspoon chopped fresh thyme

½ teaspoon crushed red pepper flakes

18 medium Pacific oysters, shucked and bottom shells reserved

Rock salt, for serving

6 lemon wedges, for garnish

Preheat the oven to 375°F.

Heat a sauté pan over medium-high heat. Add 2 tablespoons of the olive oil. Take the black trumpet mushrooms and sauté them lightly, seasoning them with salt and black pepper. When the mushrooms have given off their juices, remove from the heat. When they are cool, chop them up fine. Combine the chopped mushrooms with the bread crumbs, Parmesan, parsley, and 6 tablespoons of the remaining olive oil in a medium bowl. Reserve.

Heat the remaining 4 tablespoons olive oil in a sauté pan over medium heat. Add the chorizo and render the fat from the sausage, breaking up the meat into small pieces. Remove the sausage from the pan and reserve. Remove all but 2 tablespoons of the fat from the pan.

Add the onion, celery, and leek to the pan and cook until translucent. Add the garlic and cook just until the garlic gives off its aroma. Add the flour, whisking to combine. Deglaze the pan with the sherry, scraping up all the little bits that have accumulated. Add the cream and bring to a simmer.

Next, add the spinach and cook until it wilts. Return the sausage to the pan. Over medium heat, reduce the sausage mixture by half, or until well thickened. Add the white pepper, thyme, and red pepper flakes. Salt to taste.

Return the oysters to their shells and place on a rimmed baking sheet. Dollop each with a spoonful of the sausage mixture, then top with the mushroom mixture. Bake the oysters until the topping is golden brown and the sausage mixture is bubbling, 10 to 15 minutes.

Serve the oysters immediately on warmed plates with a layer of rock salt to keep the oysters upright. Garnish the plates with lemon wedges.

ALASKAN FISHERMEN'S HALIBUT

This straightforward recipe came right from the source: a halibut fisherman shared this recipe with us and said this is fishermen's favorite way to cook halibut when they're out on the boat in the cold waters off Alaska. Anders said it's become one of his go-to recipes when camping, and all his friends request it. There's something about eating outdoors or at sea that makes you want the rich, cheesy gooiness. The original recipe calls for a jar of Alfredo sauce, but if you're not on a fishing boat, we really recommend you just make up the Alfredo beforehand, even if you're going camping. This is an easy cheater Alfredo that still takes no more than a few minutes.

SERVES 4

Alfredo Sauce
8 tablespoons (1 stick) unsalted butter
One 8-ounce package cream cheese, at room temperature
1 cup half-and-half
½ cup grated Parmesan cheese

Kosher salt and freshly cracked black pepper
One 2-pound thick halibut fillet, skinned
8 ounces pepper Jack cheese, grated

Preheat the oven to 350°F, if making at home.

Heat the butter in a small saucepan over medium-low heat. Whisk in the cream cheese and half-and-half and cook until slightly thickened. Remove from the heat and whisk in the Parmesan. Set aside the Alfredo sauce or, if making a day ahead, place in a sealed container and refrigerate.

Place the halibut in a 12 x 12-inch disposable cake pan. Season well with salt and pepper. Pour the Alfredo sauce over the top of the fish and sprinkle with the pepper Jack.

Bake for 30 minutes on the middle rack of the oven, or until the halibut is cooked through and the cheese is bubbling.

NOTE: When camping, Anders covers the pan tightly with aluminum foil and sets it on a grate over the low part of the fire. You have to manage the cooking part a bit more, but the smoky flavor the fire imparts more than makes up for it.

COD POCKETS

Longtime customer Robyn told us that of all the choices available at Pike Place Fish, she often ends up with the simplest—a pound of ling- or true cod, or perhaps a couple of small snapper fillets that are transformed into a quick and delicious supper for her and her husband. She says that while Julia Child would call this *fish en papillote*, Anders, who often wraps her purchase, has dubbed it "cod pockets."

The beauty of this preparation is that with just a roll of parchment paper and a few ingredients, this dish can be prepared in minutes. Best of all, there are virtually no dishes or pans to clean after dinner. Use this recipe as a guideline. Get creative with additional seasonings and the freshest seasonal vegetables that appeal to you and your family.

SERVES 2

Baby spinach, washed and patted dry

Extra-virgin olive oil (or sesame oil for an Asian preparation)

Salt

2 lingcod fillets (about 1 pound; halibut, snapper, true cod, or other whitefish can be substituted, though sole may be too delicate)

2 to 3 cups sliced prepared vegetables, such as:

Thinly sliced leek, white part only

Sliced red, yellow, and/or orange bell peppers

Fresh chanterelle, shiitake, or cremini mushrooms, cleaned and sliced

Thinly sliced zucchini or summer squash

Fresh corn kernels

Thinly sliced fennel bulb (reserve the greens for garnish)

Freshly cracked black pepper

Chopped fresh parsley or other fresh herbs, for garnish

Preheat the oven to 400°F.

Cut 2 large pieces of parchment paper from the roll or use aluminum foil.

The pieces should be 16 to 18 inches long. Fold each piece in half lengthwise to mark the center. Unfold and lay the parchment flat on a clean work surface. Have ready a rimmed baking sheet.

Lay down the greens, such as spinach, on the parchment, covering ½ of the parchment and leaving a 1-inch border. Drizzle lightly with olive oil and sprinkle with salt. Lay a fish fillet on top of the spinach.

Start to layer the vegetables, preferably finishing with a colorful vegetable such as red bell pepper slices. Between layers, drizzle with a little olive oil and sprinkle with salt and pepper.

Fold the unfilled side of the parchment over the fish and vegetables. Begin sealing the parchment packet in one corner and folding a sealed edge all along the parchment until you're left with a small hole. Blow gently in to inflate the package a little, then finish by twisting the corner to seal the packet. Repeat with the remaining parchment, fish, and vegetables. Place the packets on the baking sheet.

Bake the packets for 15 to 20 minutes, or just until the vegetables are cooked through and the fish is opaque. Before removing from the oven, have ready warmed shallow bowls. To serve, carefully open the packets, being cautious of rising steam. Gently slide the contents off the parchment and into the bowls, including all the juices. Sprinkle with pepper and chopped parsley or other herbs before serving.

VARIATION: You may use 1 fish fillet and cook the entire pound in one packet. Increase the cooking time to 30 minutes total. You may also serve the fish directly from the packet at the table. To do so, open the packet with scissors or cut it open with a knife, being careful of the escaping steam.

BROWN BUTTER SPOT PRAWNS

We learned this amazingly simple and unbelievably fantastic preparation for spot prawns from the godfather of the Seattle restaurant scene himself, Tom Douglas. Make sure you cook the butter until it's truly brown, just shy of burning, to make sure you get the full nutty effect. It plays against the sweetness of the prawns beautifully.

SERVES 4

1 pound fresh spot prawns or other large shrimp
8 tablespoons (1 stick) unsalted butter
1 lemon
Kosher salt and freshly ground black pepper

Preheat the boiler.

Butterfly the prawns with the shell on, deveining and rinsing as you go (see page 47 for instructions on how to devein a shrimp or prawn). Pat dry and arrange on a rimmed baking sheet.

Heat the butter in a small saucepan, over low to medium heat. Cook, stirring constantly. You will see the solids drop to the bottom of the pan and begin to toast. The butter will become a light brown. Continue cooking, watching carefully, until the butter smells nutty and toasty and the color is a deep brown. Remove the pan from the heat and pour the butter into a bowl to stop the cooking.

Using a Microplane, grate the zest from the lemon, then quarter the lemon. Brush the brown butter liberally over the prawns. Sprinkle with the lemon zest and salt and pepper to taste. Broil the prawns just until they turn opaque, 2 to 3 minutes. Season with salt and pepper and serve with a squeeze of lemon.

ROCKFISH WITH TAPENADE

This rich tapenade is awesome with rockfish or snapper, but it would cozy up nicely to black cod, too.

SERVES 4

1 cup Pernod
1 cup fresh orange juice
½ cup sugar
1 cup pitted kalamata olives
2 garlic cloves
½ cup capers, drained
2 to 3 anchovy fillets
2 teaspoons fresh thyme
2 teaspoons chopped fresh basil
Extra-virgin olive oil
4 rockfish fillets, skin and pin bones removed
Kosher salt and freshly ground black pepper
1 tablespoon grated orange zest

Combine the Pernod, orange juice, and sugar in a medium saucepan. Bring to a boil over medium-high heat and cook, stirring occasionally, until reduced to a syrup, about 5 minutes.

Pour the syrup into the bowl of a food processor and add the olives, garlic, capers, anchovies, thyme, and basil. Pulse to combine. Add just enough olive oil, pulsing to incorporate, to create a chunky paste. Start off with 1 tablespoon and add more if necessary. Reserve the tapenade.

Heat 2 tablespoons olive oil in a large sauté pan over medium-high heat until hot but not smoking. Season the fillets on each side with salt and pepper. Add the fillets to the hot pan and cook for 2 to 3 minutes on each side, or until lightly browned and just cooked through. Serve each fillet topped with a dollop of tapenade and sprinkled with orange zest.

SOLE STUFFED WITH SHRIMP

Are there people in your crowd who find fish just too "fishy"? This is the dish for them. The flavors are light and delicate, and the little bundles are, yes, *pretty* set on the plate. A touch of lemon or parsley for garnish would be nice. For the sole, you can use wild-caught Pacific Dover sole, flounder, petrale sole, or sand dab.

SERVES 4 TO 6

2 tablespoons extra-virgin olive oil, plus more for drizzling

1 medium onion, diced

2 carrots, diced

1 pound small white shrimp, peeled and deveined

Kosher salt and freshly ground black pepper

3 tablespoons dry sherry or white wine

½ cup half-and-half

2 tablespoons fresh lemon juice

1 tablespoon dried tarragon

2 tablespoons chopped fresh parsley

½ cup dried bread crumbs

3 pounds sole fillets

Preheat the oven to 375°F.

Heat a medium sauté pan over medium heat. Add the olive oil, then the onion and carrots and cook, stirring, for 8 to 10 minutes, or until the vegetables are soft but not brown. Increase the heat to medium-high. Add shrimp to the pan and season with salt and pepper. Cook for 2 minutes more, or until shrimp are *just* pink. Add the sherry and deglaze the pan, scraping up any caramelized bits from the bottom of the pan. Remove the mixture from the heat and set aside to cool.

Combine the half-and-half, lemon juice, tarragon, parsley, bread crumbs, and shrimp mixture in the bowl of a food processor. Pulse just to combine. Taste for salt and pepper and adjust the seasoning.

Lay the sole fillets out flat on a work surface. Divide the mixture among the fillets, spooning the filling just off center on the fillets. Gently roll up each fillet to encase the filling.

Place the stuffed fillets in an oiled 13 x 9-inch baking dish. Drizzle the tops with olive oil and sprinkle with salt and pepper. Cover with aluminum foil and bake for 30 to 35 minutes, or until the fillets are opaque and the stuffing is heated through.

NUT-CRUSTED TILAPIA

Sustainably farmed tilapia is both an economical and extremely approachable fish with a sweet, mild flesh that even picky eaters can get behind. Here tilapia fillets are dusted with finely chopped nuts, then run through a hot pan. Jaison serves this dish with a spicy salsa, but we keep it simple here and substitute a wedge of lemon. After ten minutes, dinner is ready.

SERVES 4

1 cup pecans

1 cup whole milk

1 cup all-purpose flour

1½ pounds tilapia fillets

Kosher salt and freshly ground black pepper

Canola oil

1 lemon, cut into wedges

Finely chop the pecans in a food processor or with a sharp chef's knife. Place in a shallow bowl. Place the milk and flour in separate shallow bowls.

Season both sides of the tilapia well with salt and pepper. Dredge the fillets first in the flour, shaking off the excess, then dip in the milk, and finally coat thoroughly with the nuts.

Heat a thin layer of canola oil in a large nonstick skillet over medium-high heat. Add the fillets and cook until firm, turning once, about 5 minutes in all. Serve with lemon wedges.

JAKE'S SALT-ENCRUSTED ROCKFISH

There are lots of varieties of rockfish that dot the shores of our Pacific coast. They are an affordable choice and have mild white flesh that can take a whole host of sauces. If you want to pull out all the stops, buy a whole rockfish and make this fabulous recipe. Have your friendly fishmonger gut and clean it, including removing the large thorns that were built to do harm. Baking the fish in kosher salt seasons the flesh and keeps it super moist. It looks really cool, and you get to break into the baked fish as if you're an archeologist. Serve with your go-to sauce or pick a new favorite from the Basics chapter.

SERVES 4

2 pounds kosher salt, plus more for seasoning

3 large egg whites

One 3- to 5-pound rockfish, gutted and cleaned

Flavorings, such as lemon slices; fresh herbs such as thyme, tarragon, marjoram, or basil; or finely sliced shallot

Kosher salt and freshly ground black pepper

Lemon wedges (optional)

Extra-virgin olive oil, for drizzling (optional)

Preheat the oven to 400°F.

Combine the salt and egg whites in a large bowl, and mix thoroughly.

Stuff the cavity of the fish loosely with the flavorings of your choice. Season the cavity lightly with salt and pepper.

Lay a large piece of aluminum foil on a rimmed baking sheet. Spread a layer of the salt mixture, slightly bigger than the fish, over the foil. Place the fish on the salt mixture, then cover the fish with the remaining salt mixture, packing it around the fish to seal.

Bake for 30 to 35 minutes. Remove from the oven and let cool for 3 to 5 minutes. Break the salt crust and discard. The fillets should come off the bones easily. Serve with lemon on the side and maybe a drizzle of olive oil, if desired, or with your favorite sauce.